THE
WIKI WAY
OF LEARNING

D1173648

55.00

THE
WIKI WAY
OF LEARNING

Creating Learning Experiences Using Collaborative Web Pages

MICHELE NOTARI
REBECCA REYNOLDS
SAMUEL KAI WAH CHU
BEAT DÖBELI HONEGGER

An imprint of the American Library Association

CHICAGO 2016

Extensive effort has gone into ensuring the reliability of the information in this book; however, the publisher makes no warranty, express or implied, with respect to the material contained herein.

ISBN: 978–0-8389–1378-9 (paper)

Library of Congress Cataloging-in-Publication Data
Names: Notari, Michele, editor. | Reynolds, Rebecca B., 1974- editor. | Chu, Samuel (Samuel Kai Wah), editor. | Honegger, Beat Döbeli, editor.
Title: The wiki way of learning : creating learning experiences using collaborative Web pages / [edited by] Michele Notari, Rebecca Reynolds, Samuel Kai Wah Chu, Beat Döbeli Honegger.
Description: Chicago : ALA Editions, an imprint of the American Library Association, 2016. | Includes bibliographical references and index.
Identifiers: LCCN 2015043286 | ISBN 9780838913789 (print : alk. paper)
Subjects: LCSH: Internet in education. | Wikis (Computer science) | Group work in education.
Classification: LCC LB1044.87 .W488 2016 | DDC 371.33/44678—dc23 LC record available at http://lccn.loc.gov/2015043286

Cover design by Alejandra Diaz.

Text composition by Dianne M. Rooney in the Chaparral, Gotham, and Bell Gothic typefaces.

♾ This paper meets the requirements of ANSI/NISO Z39.48-1992 (Permanence of Paper).

Printed in the United States of America

20 19 18 17 16   5 4 3 2 1

Contents

MARK GUZDIAL

Foreword

Wikis in Collaborative Learning: Exploring the Role of Authority and Invention

I WAS DELIGHTED TO BE INVITED TO WRITE THIS INVITATION TO the volume, *The Wiki Way of Learning*. I have not worked in collaborative learning for several years, so I was pleased that the authors saw useful connections between my work and theirs. I was also delighted to have the opportunity to reflect on our work exploring wikis for learning, with some degree of separation.

STARTING OUT: ARE ALL THREADS CONSIDERED EQUAL?

I became interested in wikis for education as a result of earlier work in collaborative learning. For several years at Georgia Tech, my colleagues and I were exploring a tool called CaMILE (Collaborative and Multimedia Interactive Learning Environment). CaMILE was at first a Macintosh stand-alone application, and later became a web application. Basically, CaMILE supported threaded discussion lists, with some minor supports for multimedia content.

When we moved CaMILE to the Web in the late 1990s, an accident of implementation became an interesting feature to explore. Each individual threaded discussion had its own unique URL. This feature allowed us to link to a threaded discussion space from any particular content of interest to students. For example, a page describing a homework assignment could be linked to a threaded discussion space for questions and comments about that assignment. In a list of problems for students to use in reviewing for an exam, each problem could be linked to its own threaded discussion space for students to use in collaboratively solving the problem and comparing solutions. We called this "anchored collaboration," because the collaboration space was anchored to something to talk about. It was unusual in the early days of the Web to think about collaboration spaces linked to items, while it is commonplace today in blogging, and in services such as Reddit and Slashdot.

Jennifer Turns and I did a comparative study of two sets of classes to understand the impact of anchored collaboration. One set of classes used CaMILE with anchored collaborative discussions, and the other set of classes used USENET discussion groups, which were a separate discussion space and not anchored. The USENET discussion groups supported threaded talk, but not tied to any particular topic. The classes we studied were on the same or similar subjects, and were all at the same undergraduate level (e.g., students would take these courses all in their first or second year). What we found was that the anchored discussions tended to be longer (e.g., had more commentators and more notes posted) while still staying on-topic (Gudzial and Turns, 2000). Our claim was that the anchoring helped students to figure out the role for the collaboration, and kept all the related discussion in the same thread. Since we believe in the power of discussion to support learning, we would predict that *more* discussion *on-topic* was likely to result in more learning.

But as we analyzed our data, we recognized another important attribute about the anchors. All the anchors were created by the *teacher,* the authority figure in the course. Only the teacher could create an anchor (something that students cared about, linked from the home page of the course) and link it to some CaMILE discussion. That left us unsure about our claim. The anchored discussions were not just *anchored.* They were *highlighted* (by selection and reference) by the teacher. Were the longer, on-topic threads a result of the anchoring, or a result of responding to the recommendations of an authority figure?

Within the technology of CaMILE, there wasn't an easy way to test the question of anchoring versus authority. But then, my students and I discovered Ward Cunningham's WikiWikiWeb. Here was a technology in which all authors have the same authority (i.e., all words, all pages, look the same), have the same rights to create pages with the same visibility, and discussions could develop on or around any page. In a wiki, no one can tell if you're the teacher.

FROM AUTHORITY TO FLEXIBILITY

We started developing the Swiki (Squeak Wiki) in 1997, and Jeff Rick completely rewrote the code and made it his own in the following years. As we used the Swiki in less technical contexts (still many years before Wikipedia and common understanding of a "wiki"), we looked for a name that didn't involve explaining Hawaiian words. One of the teaching assistants called it a "CoWeb" for "Collaborative Website," and we used that with our less technical audiences. To all the computer science classes, it was still a "Wwiki."

We never did try to measure the amount of discussion from teacher-created pages (as anchors for discussions) versus student-created pages, because the answer was obvious from daily use. Discussions created by the teacher were *far* more likely to be visited and populated than discussions started by students. Students could tell (by tone, by explicit signature, by location in the site) which pages were written by teachers. In fact, most attempts at student-created discussions went without a single response, and those attempts were fairly rare. Our Swikis still reflected the authority structure of the classroom. For the most part, the teacher directed the students' attention, and the students took those cues to direct their attention.

What we discovered as we made Swikis available across campus was perhaps even more interesting—an enormous diversity of applications were invented by the faculty and teaching assistants around campus (Gudzial, Rick, and Kehoe, 2001). This was a striking result. The history of educational technology development is rife with interventions that don't get adopted, barely get adopted, or get adopted and used for only a small percentage of their potential applications. The Swikis were not only being adopted across campus, but a surprising variety of applications were invented for their use.

Today, when most people think "wiki" they think "Wikipedia." Creating an encyclopedia is a clear application for wikis. Our Swiki-using faculty invented such interventions as:

- A glossary of medical terms (e.g., for diseases and for bones in the body), developed across several semesters
- An annotated bibliography for a research group
- Exam review questions with a collaborative space for sharing answers
- A text-based adventure game

Swiki evolved rapidly during the first few years of its use, in response to requests from students, teachers, and teaching assistants (Gudzial, Rick, and Kerimbaev, 2000). We moved away from some of the original WikiWiki ideas. For example, we created the ability for users to "lock" pages (anyone with a particular password could unlock and edit the page). That was important, for both students and teachers, so that pages containing details like homework assignment specifications could be trusted as coming only from an authoritative source. In this way, Swiki became a wiki engine designed explicitly for classroom use.

THE DEEPER QUESTION OF WIKIS IN EDUCATION

Studies of educational uses of wikis touch on deep questions about the system and practices of schooling. These questions are not unique to wikis. Wikis serve as a lens to draw attention to these issues.

Philosophers and educational researchers as far back as John Dewey have argued that schooling should be democratic. Dewey argued that a democratic people should express their individuality. Wikis are probably among the most democratic of educational interventions. Anyone can edit any page and say anything. Yet, our experience is that use of wikis still reflected power structures within the classroom. Most classrooms are not democracies—the teacher runs the classroom, and controls what expression can occur. In the Swikis, what the teacher did was more valued than any student's contribution, and what the teacher posted or created was paid the most attention. It is not really surprising that the technology *reflected* the classroom structure—wikis are just a technology. They don't change the nature of students and teachers, but they give us a lens to see it. Is it a problem that classrooms are not more democratic? That question existed before wikis, but wikis make the question more visible.

As an educational technology, wikis are unusual for their rate of adoption and for the creative applications that teachers invented for them. As a contrast, consider that tablet computers are being adopted at a rapid rate today, but new uses are rarely being invented for them. New education applications of tablet computers for learning require literally creating new "apps." Creating new apps requires knowledge and skill for application development. Wikis can be adapted for new uses with little technical knowledge or skills.

Why do wikis inspire the invention of new applications by teachers? In general, what features of any technology inspire teachers to invent with it? A possibility is that a successfully adapted technology is one that extends an existing pedagogical tool. One of our teachers once called the wiki a "shared whiteboard." They feel like a familiar medium, with the added advantage of being shared on the Web. Do wikis get adopted for new applications because there is a sense of familiarity about them?

Wikis in their current forms are primarily textual media, and they are inherently public. Everyone can see everyone else's pages. Uses of wikis in schools, then, are a form of writing across the curriculum. Even if the wiki is being used in computer science or engineering classes, its use turns the students' activities into a public form of communication. Thus, the wiki is a *modern* Internet technology that serves to enforce some of the *oldest* goals of liberal education: basic literacy and the ability to communicate to the public.

WHAT WE DON'T KNOW ABOUT WIKIS IN EDUCATION

There is still much to learn about the role of wikis in learning and teaching. Teachers want to know what the best practices are for the use of wikis to support learning in the classroom. What does it mean to *teach* with a wiki, as an analogy to teaching with a whiteboard or a PowerPoint slide show?

For students, interaction through a wiki is different than other forums for learning. Unlike the classroom, a wiki is a written medium, and is highly distributed. Every enrolled student can be contributing (reading and writing) in the wiki, all at the same time. Students have enormous freedom in the wiki. It's less structured than even a threaded discussion space. How do students perceive these affordances? Do they use them well in order to support learning? Should we be teaching students how to use a wiki well?

I hope that this book serves as a guide toward some of these questions. The authors of this volume are exploring the range of questions related to how we think about wikis for learning and how to use them well. I am sure that you will come away from this volume with new appreciation for the power of wikis to support education.

REFERENCES

Guzdial, Mark, and Jennifer Turns. 2000. "Effective Discussion through a Computer-Mediated Anchored Forum." *Journal of the Learning Sciences* 9, no. 4: 437–69.

Guzdial, Mark, Jochen Rick, and Colleen Kehoe. 2001. "Beyond Adoption to Invention: Teacher-Created Collaborative Activities in Higher Education." *Journal of the Learning Sciences* 10, no. 3: 265–79.

Guzdial, Mark, Jochen Rick, and Bolot Kerimbaev. 2000. "Recognizing and Supporting Roles in CSCW." In *Proceedings of the 2000 ACM Conference on Computer Supported Cooperative Work—CSCW '00*, 261–68.

Introduction

PLANNING PROJECTS AND SOLVING PROBLEMS COLLABORATIVELY are crucial skills nowadays, and both require managing the information flood, being able to understand different perspectives, and working with different digital tools. *The Wiki Way of Learning* focuses on creating and managing learning processes using collaborative technologies. The book provides a theoretical approach along with hands-on examples about how to set up, run, and evaluate collaborative technology-enhanced learning lessons and curricula from the primary school level to adult education.

The introductory chapters focus on the theoretical background of participative technologies, the archetypical properties of wikis for collaboration, and the concept of higher-order learning in the form of knowledge building and learning in the field of tension between open minds and openness in education.

The following chapters underpin and illustrate the theoretical findings with practical examples of different uses of wikis from primary school education to courses on the university level around the world. The book also addresses how wikis can help structure and enhance collaboration in project-based learning settings with over 100 participants, how wikis can be used in German, history and science education, issues of evaluation and assessment of student learning in wikis, and what is the added value of the use of a wiki when a whole school uses the same wiki. Practical and pragmatic guidelines are offered addressing these themes. Finally some hands-on hints are given to teachers and lecturers about how to start their projects and lessons using wikis for collaboration.

TARGET AUDIENCE FOR THIS BOOK

The book is aimed primarily at lecturers and teachers at all levels who want to promote collaboration using digital media, and who are looking for inspiration, theoretical backgrounds, successful practical examples, and specific details regarding the design and implementation of technology-enhanced collaboration.

BEAT DÖBELI HONEGGER
AND MICHELE NOTARI

1
The Wiki Principle

WHY ARE WIKIS RELEVANT?

Wikipedia (http://wikipedia.org), Wikileaks (http://wikileaks.org), WikiPlag (http://de.wikiplag.wikia.com/wiki/WikiPlag_Wiki). What began as a tool to document software projects more than fifteen years ago has developed, since that time, into a widespread application for the collaborative creation and editing of texts. Thanks to a few simple basic principles, volunteers can create the world's largest encyclopedia together, Wikipedia. More and more companies and interest groups are now using wikis or wiki-like tools for the joint preparation of documents.

The first wiki was launched on the Internet by software developer Ward Cunningham in 1995. It was intended to be used for software development, as a documentation tool for design patterns, and became a popular tool in the developer community. The inspiration for the name *wiki* came from the label "wiki wiki" on the express buses at the Hawaii airport, which means "quickly, quickly" in Hawaiian. Ward Cunningham's wiki was by far the easiest and fastest tool for editing web pages at that time.

With this quick and easy way of editing web pages, Cunningham fulfilled World Wide Web (WWW) inventor Berners-Lee's original vision of collaborative hypertext. At the beginning of his work on the WWW, Berners-Lee had already foreseen that web pages could be both read and edited with a browser (Berners-Lee and Fischetti, 1999). However, in the first phase of the Web, the roles of producing and consuming on the content of web pages continued to be strictly separated.

In retrospect, this first phase of the World Wide Web is now known as Web 1.0. Wikis can be seen as a pioneer and archetype of Web 2.0, which is the second phase of the WWW. In Web 2.0, the roles of producing and consuming content are merged to become "prosuming." The Internet is increasingly being used as a substitute for local computers and for storage media. Instead of clearly defined programs, services that continuously evolve are used in a network (O'Reilly, 2005). Some experts postulate that these technical changes are accompanied by a cultural shift toward a higher level of cooperation. Don Tapscott and Anthony D. Williams have described such forms of cooperation and its consequences for different areas of business and society in their books *Wikinomics* (2006) and *Macro-Wikinomics* (2010).

As regards the significance of the wiki as the *archetype of a new tool and a new approach to the Internet,* only a small part of this book will be devoted to the concrete wiki tool. Technology and concrete tools are subject to constant change. The initial unique concepts of wikis, meanwhile, have found their way into many other tools and web services. What remains from the concrete tool are the wiki's inherent universal characteristics, which are very suitable for teaching and learning in an information society, and will be described herein.

WHAT MAKES A WIKI?

In a speech about the design principles of wiki, the wiki inventor Ward Cunningham asked rhetorically: "How can so little do so much?" (Cunningham, 2006). He explained, from his perspective, the design principles of the wiki based on the shortest known program, which implements the basic functions of a wiki in 222 characters of Perl-Code.

```
#!/usr/bin/perl

use CGI':all';path_info=~/\w+/;$_='grep -1 $& *.'h1($&)
.escapeHTML$t=param(t)

||'dd<$&';open F,">$&";print F$t;s/htt\S+|([A-Z]\w+)
{2,}/a{href,$&},$&/eg;

print header,pre"$_<form>",submit,textarea t,$t,9,70[1]
```

This snippet is not easy even for computer scientists to interpret. It visualizes one of the most important wiki features: a reduction to the essentials. With these 222 characters, the basic functions of a wiki are wholly defined.

An easier definition of the wiki for those who are not computer scientists is as follows:

> A Wiki is a web service with version control on the Internet, in which
> everyone can create and modify web pages, link them as hypertexts,
> and be informed about content changes on request, without additional
> tools or HTML knowledge. (Based on Döbeli Honegger, 2007)

Currently, over 100 Wiki variants are available.[2] They have inherited most of the basic ideas of Ward Cunningham's original wiki, but offer more or less degrees of additional functionality, and differ in the technical details that are most relevant to their operation, but not to the use of the wikis. The most common wiki features are:

Full-text search. All pages of a wiki can be searched in full text.

Ref-by-function. On each wiki page, other referenced pages of the wiki are shown.

List of changes. A wiki server delivers a list of the most recently added or modified pages. This information is also available as an RSS feed or by periodic e-mails.

Version control. A wiki server logs every change to a wiki page and provides comparisons between the different versions or lists them on a complete page history.

User management. Some Wiki servers require user registration and record the name of the user who creates or modifies the page.

Wikis and Wiki-Like Tools

Between 1995 and 2000, a wiki was practically the only way to edit a web page directly in the browser. Today, many web services allow the direct manipulation of websites, and are usually even easier to use than traditional wikis. In particular, a class of *Wiki-like tools* has been developed. These tools largely forego the hypertext functions and instead focus on the work of simple linear texts. Table 1.1 shows the relevant differences between classic wikis and newer wiki-like tools.

Read and Editing Modes

At first glance, a wiki page is hardly different from a traditional website (see figure 1.1). Most of them have a navigation bar with important links on one

TABLE 1.1

Differences between classic wikis and wiki-like tools.

Properties	Classic Wikis	Wiki-like Tools
Document structure	Hypertext consisting of multiple documents linked to one another	Single linear document
Read and edit	Separate	Together
Versioning	After each save	After each letter typed
Presentation of page history	Comparison between different versions	Film-like playback of development process
Dealing with editing conflicts	Preventative hard or soft blocks Attempts to resolve conflict when editing conflict occurs No conflict resolution	No editing conflicts
WYSIWYG-Editor	Partial	Yes

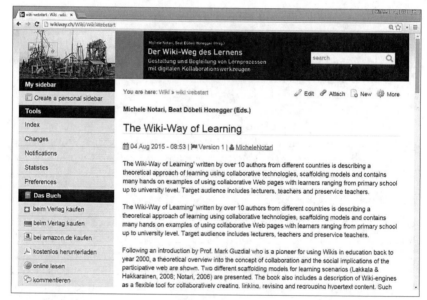

FIGURE 1.1

A Wiki page in view mode (http://wikiway.ch).

The left sidebar contains important links and the toolbox that allows users to create a new topic, browse the index, search, view changes, settings, and statistics or add the page to the RSS feed. The central part of the page includes the actual content consisting of text, images, or other content. The "Edit"- or "Modify"-buttons at the left top of the page and in the navigation bar at the bottom enable the user to switch from the view to the edit mode (figure 1.2).

edge of the page, with the actual information in the central area of the page. This look is called the view mode.

The page can be recognized as a wiki page only at second glance. Somewhere on the page is a link or button labelled "Modify" or "Edit." In a classic Wiki, the page will enter an editing mode upon clicking this link or button (see figure 1.2). The first wikis did not have a graphical text editor. All formatting and graphical elements had to be entered with special codes, as shown in figure 1.2. More modern Wikis provide a graphical editing mode, as is common today in various word processing programs (see figure 1.3).

FIGURE 1.2

A wiki page in user mode (http://wikiway.ch).

The center of the page includes the editor, in which the users can modify the content with the help of an integrated text editor. The buttons at the bottom of the page allow the user to save and close with or without notification, to save while editing, to cancel, and to preview the page. The editor used in this example does not provide any graphical editing support (WYSIWYG). The users have to use special codes to enter graphical or formatting elements.

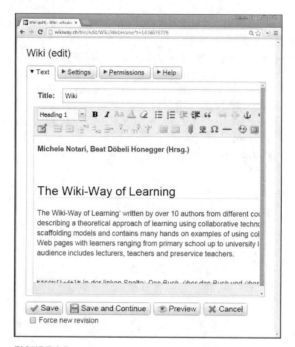

FIGURE 1.3

A wiki page in graphical edit mode (WYSIWYG)
(http://wikiway.ch).

The editor in the center of the page enables users to modify the
content with the help of graphical elements to format the text
and enter images or other elements. The bar on the top of the
editor contains the symbols that have to be clicked to trigger the
corresponding text-processing functions. The bottom of the page
contains buttons with the same various save, cancel, and preview
functions like the text edit mode (figure 1.2).

Although most wikis today provide a graphical editing mode, the text
editing mode still enjoys great popularity among wiki professionals. Since the
main formatting rules are well known and there is little to format, working
in the text mode is usually faster, because you can enter the commands using
the keyboard and not have to change continuously between the mouse and
keyboard.

The editing of a wiki page is completed by storing or discarding the
changes made, after which the user is returned to the view mode.

Wiki-like tools usually do not distinguish between these two modes. You
are always in the edit mode, and the pages can be modified at any time and by
multiple users simultaneously (see figure 1.5).

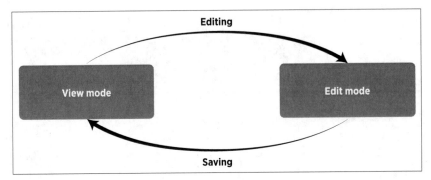

FIGURE 1.4
Switching between view mode and edit mode in a classic wiki.

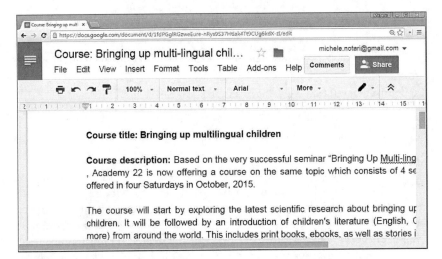

FIGURE 1.5
Edit mode of a wiki-like tool.

The graphical editor (WYSIWYG) in the center of the page allows multiple users to simultaneously modify the content with the help of the graphical text-processing functions. Unlike a normal wiki, a Wiki-like tool is always in the edit mode.

Version Management and Editing Conflicts

In a classic wiki, switching between view and edit modes (see figure 1.4) also serves as the basis for version management and for dealing with potential editing conflicts. The active saving system in a classic wiki means that new versions of the page can be stored. With version management, users can go back to each saved version, and can compare several versions of the same page (see figure 1.6).

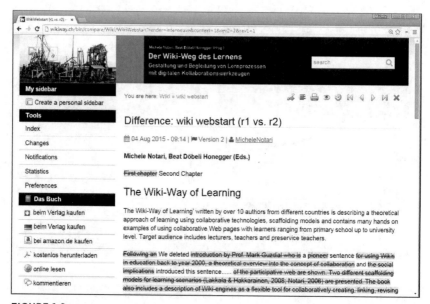

FIGURE 1.6

Comparison of different versions in a typical wiki.

The page shows a typical feature of version management used to compare different versions of the document stored in the wiki.

Wiki-like tools lack not only the switch between viewing and editing modes, but very often also lack an explicit command to save the document. Wiki-like tools automatically save after every single change in the document (i.e., after every single keystroke), but they do not give clear information about when the editing process has been completed. Different wiki-like tools handle this in different ways. While some tools show the history of a document, much like a film playback, others attempt to recognize and display different versions based on temporal interruptions (see figure 1.7).

Since every single letter change is saved by the wiki-like tools and is tracked in the web browsers where the relevant document is displayed, simultaneous editing of the document becomes possible. In classic wikis, editing conflicts occur when multiple users access a document at the same time, because one user's saving process might overwrite the changes made by another. Classic wikis use different strategies to tackle this problem. Some of them lock the document from further editing when one user enters the edit mode. This prevents an editing conflict, but also rules out the possibility of simultaneous editing. Other classic wikis only warn the users about a possible editing conflict upon saving, and leave the next steps to the users themselves. A third

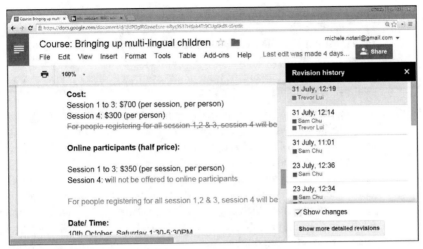

FIGURE 1.7
Version management in a wiki-like tool (Google Docs).

The document's content is displayed in the editor at the center of the page. The bar on top of the editor contains a function to display all the versions of the documents saved in drive. The bar on the right side of the editor visualizes the revision history, including date and time of saving, user name of the editor, and the type of change.

type of classic wiki tries to integrate the changes from different users into the document automatically, while indicating potential conflicts directly.

WHAT MAKES WIKIS SPECIAL?

> *The program has an attitude. The program wants everyone to be an author. So, the program slants in favor of authors at some inconvenience to readers.* (Leuf and Cunningham, 2001)

Just like all tools, Wikis influence our thoughts and actions. Tools do not stipulate that we use them in particular ways, but they would suggest so. We would be reluctant to use a hammer to paint the wall, or a screwdriver to drive in a nail. Similarly, wikis also suggest certain ways of use. Wikis focus more on the content and less on the format of a text. The development process is of equal weight as the result. Wikis emphasize three design principles: *simplicity, openness,* and *user activation* (Döbeli Honegger, 2005).

Wikis are simple. The first principle in the invention of wikis was simplicity. Ward Cunningham described wikis as "the simplest functional online database."[3] With his invention of wikis in 1995, Cunningham massively simplified the editing of web pages and set a foundation for future online text editors. Wikis require neither special programs nor browser applets, nor detailed technical knowledge such as HTML syntax rules. What they require is only a web browser, which is available on any computer. The graphical editor becomes available by simply clicking a button, and the most essential design options can be defined with only a few special characters.

Wikis are open. The first wiki created by Cunningham did not have any reading or writing restrictions. Cunningham assumed that any possible vandalism in a wiki could be contained easily by the majority of the well-intended users. This has been confirmed, by and large, to this day. Wikis do need to be protected from automatically registered advertisements. This is particularly true for highly exposed wikis such as Wikipedia, which requires additional protection mechanisms. Otherwise, though, an open wiki can be easily operated without the risk of being defaced or abused.

Wikis are welcoming. Wikis are not primarily intended for passive consumption. They encourage visitors to take part in the writing process. This is achieved mainly by the already mentioned design principles of simplicity and openness. Be it a typo on an external page or the submission of your own idea, wikis allow for an immediate correction, or the extension of a text, without facing big hurdles, consent, or preliminary work from a third party. The focus on active participation goes so far in favor of active users that the drawbacks for passive users are tolerated. Due to the additional options for editing and the limited choices of layouts, wiki pages are often less attractive than read-only pages—a wiki feature which is often criticized.

Classic wikis and wiki-like tools differ from other word-processing programs that allow for the creation of perfect-looking documents, due to the fact that classic wikis and wiki-like tools usually place more emphasis on the content and the editing process, rather than the format and the end product.

Wikis are content-focused. You can certainly format and structure texts with a wiki. Headings, as well as numbered and unnumbered lists, are available in practically all wikis, and characters can be made bold or italic. The simple capabilities are there, but so far most wikis do not offer complex formatting or design capabilities, since wikis focus more on the content and less on the format of a text.

Wikis are process-oriented. The link available on each wiki page for editing is an expression of the idea that a text is never finished and can be modified at any time. Version management of wikis provides access to all the development stages of a text, from the beginning to the current date. In addition, specialized wiki pages, as well as RSS feeds and e-mail alerts, make keeping up with the changes easier.

HYPOTHESES

The references with the numbering system a00000 refer to the hypotheses in "Beats Biblionetz," http://beat.doebe.li/bibliothek/index.html. Some links lead to sites written in German, while others connect to English articles and references:

a00618 http://doebe.li/a00618
 Wiki promotes motivation in education and training
a00619 http://doebe.li/a00619
 Wiki promotes the ability to assume responsibility in
 education and training
a00653 http://doebe.li/a00653
 Wiki promotes media competence of students in school
a00709 http://doebe.li/a00709
 Features of good teaching 02: intensive use of learning time
a00742 http://doebe.li/a00742
 Revision of texts promotes their quality
a00732 http://doebe.li/a00732
 Writing on the computer facilitates the revision of texts
a00890 http://doebe.li/a00890
 Collaborative writing can promote learning
a00889 http://doebe.li/a00889
 Wiki is very suitable for collaborative writing
a00984 http://doebe.li/a00984
 Learning is an active process
a00985 http://doebe.li/a00985
 Learning is a self-directed process
a00986 http://doebe.li/a00986
 Learning is a constructive process
a00987 http://doebe.li/a00987
 Learning is a situational process
a00988 http://doebe.li/a00988
 Learning is a social process
a01138 http://doebe.li/a01138
 Students write longer texts on a computer than by hand
a01139 http://doebe.li/a01139
 Writing on the computer can promote motivation in writing

WHY ARE WIKIS SUITABLE FOR LEARNING?

After a certain time, the didactic potential of wikis for the construction of hypertexts in universities (Guzdial, Rick, and Kehoe, 2001) and school environments (Notari, 2003) was discovered. Speaking very generally, there are two reasons why wikis are suitable for the teaching and learning processes of the twenty-first century: they fit the current constructivist understanding of learning, as well as the requirements of the emerging information society.

As Johannes Moskaliuk describes in more detail in this book, learning is today understood as an active (a00984), self-directed (a00985), constructive (a00986), social (a00988), and situational (a00987) process. Based on this moderate constructivist view (e.g., Vygotsky, 1978; Piaget, 1977; Reinmann and Mandl, 2001), learning takes place in an active way, where new knowledge is generated in social contexts and specific situations. Wikis can support this process exactly, because the inviting, open, and process-oriented nature of wikis encourages the joint construction of new knowledge assets.

The growing amount of data and the complexity of our information society means there is an increasing need for wiki-like tools and team-oriented, multi-perspective work. More new, innovative solutions can be worked out in interdisciplinary teams on the basis of questioning existing approaches and supplementing them.

In the following, the potential of wikis for teaching and learning processes will be considered in detail, based on the quoted definition of wiki below:

> A Wiki is a web Service with version control (e) on the Internet (f), in which anyone (b) with no additional tools (g) or HTML knowledge
>
> (h) can create (a), or modify (c) web pages and link them as hypertexts
>
> (d), and can be informed about content changes upon request. (Based on Döbeli Honegger, 2007)

(a) Create

Web pages can be created quickly and easily with a wiki. Teachers can provide information materials, assignments, and lists of links on the wiki without much technical effort. The much greater potential lies in the fact that students can also develop the content. A wiki is very suitable for presentations and the documentation of student work, and has several advantages over traditional means of learning:

> **Organization.** Texts presented in a digital way can nowadays be easily accessible in every classroom. Computer fonts are easier to read than handwriting, which simplifies the mutual reading of created texts.

Language. Writing on a wiki means writing with a computer. Numerous studies show that students are sometimes more motivated to write (a01139; Warschauer, 2009) and produce lengthier texts (a01138; Schaumburg, 2006; Warschauer, 2009) using a computer than by hand. Many other reports about wiki projects also support this hypothesis of motivation enhancement (a00618; Osman-El Sayed, 2006; Paus-Hasebrink et al., 2007).

Content. When students express and present their knowledge in a wiki, they also actively examine the topic. This corresponds to the constructivist idea of the process for building one's own knowledge structure. Working in a wiki means active learning time, which is seen as an indicator of good teaching (a00709; Meyer, 2003; Helmke, 2005). In this respect, it is advantageous that wikis focus more on the content than the format of texts, because it is less likely for students to lose themselves in a variety of display options.

Media education. Numerous aspects of media production can be experienced and addressed when working on a wiki, such as appropriate formulations and presentations, plagiarism, copyright issues, and proper citations (a00653).

(b) Anyone

Wikis allow for the collaborative creation of texts (a00889). Indeed, on a wiki, collaboration is more heavily weighted than the contribution of an individual person. Although the author of each part of a text can be cited, this feature is more or less hidden. The main focus is the text; not the creator or author. As digital tools to support group work, wikis offer the following potential advantages:

Language. A text is written by two or more students together, and they can jointly discuss and solve language problems (Kochan, 2006).

Content. The common creation of a text promotes not only linguistic exchanges, but also collaboration on substantive aspects (a00890; Azevedo, 2005).

Media education. In addition to general teamwork and social skills, the increasingly important competence in joint text production is also practiced. In this regard, the learner's assumption of responsibility and independence is encouraged (a00619; Paus-Hasebrink et al., 2007).

(c) Modify

Writing with a computer generally makes the revision of content easier (a00732). Learners can revise their own and others' texts more easily and more quickly than on paper. Wikis support the perpetual revision process through version management, and using the usual options such as RSS or e-mail, whereby the users can be informed about any changes on the wiki. This has the following potential advantages:

Content. The revision of one's own or another person's text encourages discussion of the topic. Content is repeatedly addressed and understanding is deepened (a00890; Azevedo, 2005; Mak and Coniam, 2008). In this case, certain content is addressed again within a certain time interval, which shows that wikis support the idea of a spiral curriculum, as suggested by Jerome Bruner (1960).

Language. The revision of text improves its linguistic quality (a00742; Warschauer, 2009).

(d) Link as Hypertexts

Like all hypertext systems, wikis allow different contents (i.e., text excerpts) to be linked to one another. Contents can be presented not only in a linear way, but also as a network. This again has the following potential for learning:

Content. Learners are encouraged to find sensible connections, which is another opportunity for them to actively examine their own or another's texts. It is still unclear whether hypertexts alone are conducive to learning (f00049). Among others, Schulmeister (1996) points out that even with hypertexts, creation is more conducive to learning than simply consumption.

Content. Hypertext documents are particularly suitable for certain types of texts such as reference books, argument trees, and decision histories.

Content. Hypertexts can promote a multi-perspective view and approach.

Content. When a user creates or reads a wiki text, serendipitous learning can occur. Users click through the hyperlinks, and read content and themes that were not originally sought, but which are helpful in solving the original problems (a01167; Moskaliuk and Kimmerle, 2008; Bremer, 2012).

Media education. Through their own activities, the learners will experience the advantages and drawbacks of hypertexts.

(e) With Version Control

Wiki's version control allows all previously saved versions of a document to be retrieved. This makes it possible to view the history of a document in retrospect and conduct an analysis. Unintentional mistakes, or acts of vandalism, can also be easily discovered and undone. Version control also contributes to the learning process in the following ways:

Organization. Teachers can clearly follow the work of their students. This simplifies the management of independent work phases.

Language. Students can view the formation of their texts and analyze them retrospectively (Mak and Coniam, 2008).

Content. In addition to language development, learners can track substantive differences in their text, which allows them to gain insight into their own learning process and promotes the student's metacognitive skills (Azevedo, 2005).

(f) On the Internet and (g) with No Additional Tools

A wiki can be installed on a web server and accessed with a browser. Since browsers are now preinstalled on virtually all Internet-enabled devices, learners need not install anything further before using the wiki and can access all created content from anywhere. As such, wikis are the first services in what is today referred to as *cloud computing*. Schools do not require servers in the school building, and neither teachers nor students need to install additional software. This reduces both user hurdles and the cost of implementing digital media.

(h) No HTML Knowledge

Creating and editing web pages without HTML knowledge, and with the help of wikis, does not carry the same significance as it did in 1995. Nonetheless, it is still important that working with wikis is no more difficult than handling a word processor. Wikis do not require above-average ICT (information and communication technology) skills, and all teachers and students should be able to manage using a Wiki.

CRITICISM ON WIKI

Wikis and wiki-like tools are neither a panacea nor a sure guarantee for good teaching and learning. They also have their limits and restrictions. The following is a list of some frequently heard criticisms:

"Wikis look ugly"

Wikis usually do not look very appealing and their layout options are limited. This deters both teachers and students. If web pages are to be created, they should also look good!

Answer: In fact, most Wikis offer only rudimentary formatting options, and the overall appearance can only be changed or customized in a limited way. This is a consequence of the content-focused nature of wikis, and it has the advantage that learners focus more on the content and less on the format. For the appealing documentation of a project or similar work, other tools would be more appropriate.

"Wikis are very text-heavy"

It is usually very difficult, if not impossible, to include images, sounds and videos in a wiki in an efficient and appealing manner. This means that a wiki gives up all the multimedia potential that any other digital media tool could offer.

Answer: Until a few years ago, wikis were primarily oriented to text documents. However, the more recent wikis allow for the light integration of images, sounds, and videos. These can be stored in the wiki or linked from other web pages, and then displayed or played directly on the wiki. Direct editing of multimedia data, such as cropping images, is rarely possible in wikis, however.

"Students are not experts: their results should not be used by other students"

Students are usually not experts in the area in which they write a wiki entry. It is therefore possible that facts are explained wrongly or in an awkward way in their wiki contribution. Such pages are not suitable as learning materials for other students.

Answer: This is not a wiki-specific phenomenon, but is a consequence of collaboration. If knowledge, experience, and content are exchanged between learners, false concepts and content will also be included. However, in a wiki, errors can be corrected quickly by both teachers and students. The teachers can assign students to comment and ask about any incomprehensible contributions.

"The openness of Wiki leads to intentional vandalism"

There is a risk that individuals may intentionally include errors, delete texts, or submit inappropriate texts that are not related to the topic.

Answer: In practice, such Wiki vandalism rarely happens in smaller learning communities, and can easily be solved thanks to version management. Spam attacks are a more significant problem in bigger wikis that are open to the public.

"The openness of Wiki intimidates learners"

Inexperienced wiki users are often unable to cope with the openness and lack of structure of a wiki. They do not dare to create their own pages or to correct and expand the pages of others.

Answer: Working in a wiki is actually unusual and challenges current practices and attitudes. For this reason, instructions about working with a wiki must be introduced as precisely as possible, so that the initial timidity concerning the wiki will quickly disappear. It is therefore advisable to carry on using the Wikis multiple times, since the introductory phase only needs to be carried out once.

"A Wiki's lack of structure overburdens teachers and students"

A classic wiki has no preset structure and is "open" like a blank page. The structure of the content can and must be defined and created by the authors. This might present an additional difficulty, especially for younger learners, and might also be considered inefficient.

Answer: The teacher can define, or at least give clear instructions, for the wiki's structure. Normally, the wiki is simple and clear at the beginning of the course, but as the wiki grows along with different entries and students' work, the structure loses its clarity. To a certain extent, the learners must develop their competence in maintaining clarity. The creation of structure is an explicit part of the learning objective and assignments. In the long term, the ability to establish a meaningful structure and to modify it when necessary is important.

"A Wiki cannot be controlled"

When a wiki functions well, so much might be written on it that any attempt to control all the content would take a lot of effort, or might be impossible.

Answer: Such a development in the learning environment is mainly a good sign! When would teachers complain that their students have done too much work? In order to process the large amount of information, peer reviews, for example, can be planned.

"It is not possible to grade the content of a Wiki, because it is not clear who wrote which part of the text."

Depending on the configuration of the wiki, it might not be clear who wrote or edited a certain text. Under certain circumstances, it would be difficult or even impossible to assess individual students.

Answer: From a technical perspective, it depends on how the wiki is used and how easy it is to assign individual authorship. Students may be advised to indicate their contribution by name. This criticism reveals a dilemma in educational institutions, where performance is usually evaluated individually but where the assignment may be performed in teams.

NOTES

1. Source: http://c2.com/cgi/wiki?SigWik.
2. See www.wikimatrix.org.
3. www.wiki.org/wiki.cgi?WhatIsWiki.

REFERENCES

Azevedo, R. 2005. "Using Hypermedia as a Metacognitive Tool for Enhancing Student Learning? The Role of Self-Regulated Learning." *Educational Psychologist* 40, no. 4: 199–209. http://doebe.li/t14739.

Berners-Lee, T., and M. Fischetti. 1999. "Weaving the Web." http://doebe.li/b01866.

Bremer, C. 2012. "Wikis in der Hochschullehre." In *Wikis in Schule und Hochschule*, ed. M. Beißwenger, N. Anskeit, and N. Storrer. Glückstadt. vwh.http://doebe.li/t14117.

Bruner, J. 1960. *The Process of Education.* http://doebe.li/b00733.

Cunningham, W. 2006. "Design Principles of Wiki: How Can So Little Do So Much?" Keynote at WikiSym 2006 in Odense, Denmark. http://c2.com/doc/wikisym/WikiSym2006.pdf, http://doebe.li/t5964.

Döbeli Honegger, B. 2005. "Wiki und die starken LehrerInnen." In *Unterrichtskonzepte für informatische Bildung*, ed. S. Friedrich, 173–83. Lecture Notes in Informatics. http://doebe.li/t4624.

———. 2007. "Wiki und die starken Potenziale: Unterricht mit Wikis als virtuel-len Wandtafeln." *Web 2.0—Internet Interaktiv: Zeitschrift Computer und Unterricht* no. 66: 39–41. http://doebe.li/t07400.

Guzdial, M., J. Rick, and C. Kehoe. 2001. "Beyond Adoption to Invention: Teacher-Created Collaborative Activities in Higher Education." *Journal of the Learning Sciences* 10, no. 3. http://doebe.li/t02237.

Helmke, A. 2005. *Unterrichtsqualität, Erfassen, Bewerten, Verbessern.* Seelze: Kallmeyer.

Kochan, B. 2006. "Schreibprozess, Schreibentwicklung und Schreibwerkzeug: Theoretische Aspekte des Computergebrauchs im entfaltenden Schreibunterricht." In *Computer und Schriftspracherwerb*, ed. W. Hofmann, J. Müsseler, and H. Adolphs. http://doebe.li/t06029.

Koenig, C., A. Müller, and J. Neumann. 2007. "Wie können Wikis im E-Learning ihr Potential entfalten?" In *Wikis: Diskurse, Theorien und Anwendungen*, ed. C. Stegbauer, J. Schmidt, and K. Schönberger. Special issue of *kommunikation@gesellschaft*, 8. http://doebe.li/t07797.

Leuf, B., and W. Cunningham. 2001. *The Wiki Way: Quick Collaboration on the Web.* http://doebe.li/b01094.

Mak, B., and D. Coniam. 2008. "Using Wikis to Enhance and Develop Writing Skills among Secondary School Students in Hong Kong." *System* 36: 437–55. http://doebe.li/ t14741.

Meyer, H. 2003. "Zehn Merkmale guten Unterrichts: Empirische Befunde und didaktische Ratschläge." *Pädagogik*, no. 10: 36–43. http://doebe.li/t05689.

Moskaliuk, J., and J. Kimmerle. 2008. "Wikis in der Hochschule—Faktoren für den erfolgreichen Einsatz." eTeaching.org, November 19. http://doebe.li/t14740.

Notari, M. 2003. "Scripting Strategies in Computer Supported Collaborative Learning Environments." http://doebe.li/b02617.

O'Reilly, T. 2005. "What Is Web 2.0? Design Patterns and Business Models for the Next Generation of Software." http://oreilly.com/web2/archive/what-is-web-20.html, http://doebe.li/t11607.

Osman-El Sayed, R. 2006. *Wiki-Systeme im eLearning*. Frankfurt: Bibliothek Informatik. http://doebe.li/b03051.

Paus-Hasebrink, I., et al. 2007. "Lernen mit Web 2.0: Evaluation des Projekts Web 2.0-Klasse Zentrale Ergebnisse." http://doebe.li/t07973.

Piaget, J. 1977. *The Development of Thought: Equilibration of Cognitive Structures*. New York: Viking. http://doebe.li/b05153.

Reinmann, G., and H. Mandl. 2001. "Unterrichten und Lernumgebungen gestalten." In *Pädagogische Psychologie: Ein Lehrbuch*, ed. A. Krapp and B. Weidenmann, 613–58. Weinheim: Beltz. http://doebe.li/t03580.

Schaumburg, H. 2006. "Elektronische Textverarbeitung und Aufsatzleistung: Empirische Ergebnisse zur Nutzung mobiler Computer als Schreibwerkzeug in der Schule." *Unterrichtswissenschaft* 1: 22–45. http://doebe.li/t06852.

Schulmeister, R. 1996. *Grundlagen hypermedialer Lernsysteme*. Munich: Oldenbourg. http://doebe.li/b00225.

Tapscott, D., and A. D. Williams. 2006. *Wikinomics*. New York: Portfolio. http://doebe.li/ b03029.

———. 2010. *Macro-Wikinomics*. New York: Portfolio. http://doebe. li/b04930.

Vygotsky, L. S. 1978. *Mind in Society*. Cambridge, MA: Harvard University Press. http:// doebe.li/b01619.

Warschauer, M. 2009. "Learning to Write in the Laptop Classroom." *Writing & Pedagogy* 1, no. 1: 101–12. http://doebe.li/t14187.

JOHANNES MOSKALIUK

2

Knowledge Construction Using Wikis

Theoretical Approaches and Implications for Schools

WIKIS ENABLE AND PROMOTE THE COLLABORATIVE CONSTRUC-tion of knowledge. The main question is under what conditions can the use of wikis promise success and which psychological, educational, and socio-logical theories are suitable framework models? Therefore, I am going to pres-ent the value of wikis from a theoretical perspective and try to derive their implications for educational purposes.[1]

First, the constructivist theory of Piaget (1977) will be described, which assumes a qualitative change in cognitive schemata during the development of an individual, and defines the occurring cognitive processes in greater detail. The theory of Vygotsky (1986) will also be discussed, which emphasizes the importance of social interactions between people. This chapter shall present the further development of these concepts in the *knowledge building model* and the *cognitive apprenticeship* approach. Luhmann's social system theory (1995) will also be briefly discussed. Since a wiki and its associated community can be understood as a social system, Luhmann's theory can be applied to knowledge building with wikis. In addition, the model of Cress and Kimmerle (2008) will be presented, which integrates the views of Piaget and Luhmann and describes learning as a *coevolution* of knowledge and information. Finally, *intrinsic motivation* and *interest* will be presented as essential motivational factors.

CONSTRUCTIVISM: LEARNING AS ACTIVE CONSTRUCTION OF KNOWLEDGE

A large number of the teaching methods in schools utilize the proverbial Nuremberg funnel, in order to instill knowledge by frontal teaching. Related to this is the assumption that experiences can be shared among individuals, and knowledge can be exchanged and learned as a form of expertise regardless of one's own experiences. This is contradicted by the epistemological approach of constructivism, which assumes that learners create their own representation of their environment. What is taught does not correspond to what is actually learned, which also depends on the learners and their individual experiences. Therefore, the term *knowledge construction* is used as opposed to the terms *learning* or *knowledge acquisition*. This takes into account that the construction of knowledge is caused by individual experiences, regardless of whether that knowledge is already available to others. A transfer or funneling of knowledge independent of individual experiences and the resulting knowledge construction is not possible. Only active engagement with new content, ideas, and suggestions from others can lead to the integration of new experiences into existing knowledge.

PIAGET'S APPROACH: IMPACT OF COGNITIVE CONFLICTS

Theoretical approach: a focal point of constructivism is Jean Piaget's (1977) approach. He assumes a constant change in cognitive schemata during the course of human development. A cognitive schema structures and simplifies the environment. It is the typical way for a human to understand their environment and it organizes individual experiences (Bartlett, 1932). A schema can be formally described as the sum of the individual units of knowledge on a particular topic or issue, and the relationship among these individual units. Examples of cognitive schemata are action schemata (e.g., throwing or knocking) or schemata that can be used as an aid to classify different objects (e.g., objects to throw or to knock). Cognitive schemata structure the environment and facilitate the storage and retrieval of knowledge (Rumelhart, 1980). They reduce the complexity of the environment. Knowledge construction is the interpretation of new experiences using existing schemata and the development of new schemata over time. Existing schemata are more flexibly applied, and may be changed and adapted.

What causes knowledge construction, and the change and adaptation of cognitive schemata? Piaget assumes that people are always motivated to be in cognitive balance. If this equilibrium is disturbed by new experiences, a cognitive conflict occurs that must be resolved. In this case, the person's cognitive schemata no longer match the experiences that construct the environment, and so an adaptation to the environment is required. Therefore, the disruption of cognitive schemata from the environment triggers knowledge construction. New knowledge must be integrated into existing schemata, or the existing schemata have to be adapted and developed.

Implications for the use of wikis: the idea of cognitive conflicts as a catalyst for knowledge construction can be applied to the use of wikis in the classroom. When students read information in a wiki that does not fit into their own prior knowledge, their cognitive balance is disrupted. They are encouraged to structure or adapt their own knowledge anew, or to modify the wiki. Unlike reading a book, the learners have the opportunity to actively participate in knowledge construction. This changes the role of the teachers because they are not only brokers of learning content, who prepare didactic work and utilize the appropriate teaching method. They must also provide an environment in which students can experience and resolve cognitive conflicts. This involves creating a classroom environment that promotes critical and active engagement with the content. Wikis generate and uncover cognitive conflicts (e.g., by providing new or contradictory information), while they also provide a platform for users to actively deal with these conflicts and resolve them.

VYGOTSKY'S APPROACH: LEARNING AS A SOCIAL PROCESS

Theoretical approach: another important representative of constructivism is the Russian psychologist Lev Semenovich Vygotsky. In his approach the social interactions among learners are of great significance; that is, knowledge is socially constructed. Even thinking is understood, by Vygotsky, as a social activity and reflects the culture in which the individuals interact (Vygotsky, 1986). Learners grow into a knowledge culture. At first, they can only solve tasks and problems with the help of others, and thereby construct individual cognitive schemata over time, in order to understand their environment. According to Vygotsky, knowledge is constructed through interactions with other individuals. The constructed knowledge is initially always bound to the context in which it is acquired. Knowledge does not exist in an abstract manner as right or wrong, but depends on the social and physical context.

Scardamalia and Bereiter (2006) build upon Vygotsky's approach. With "Knowledge Building" they describe the construction of new knowledge in a knowledge society. They distinguish learning as an internal and unobservable process from knowledge building, which is the creation and modification of new knowledge that is socially shared and situated. Knowledge building takes place when the borders of a community's knowledge are reached; for example, if a class cannot explain natural phenomena with already known concepts. Scardamalia and Bereiter draw a comparison here with a scientific community that generates new knowledge and shares it with the society. They consider this form of constructivist learning as the ideal form for all levels of education and professional training.

The approach of "Cognitive Apprenticeship" (Collins, Brown and Newman, 1989) is based on Vygotsky's tradition. Here, the acquisition of cognitive skills is compared with the acquisition of skills in craft training. The authors extend this approach to learning at a school and postulate that the acquisition of cognitive skills can only take place in a social context. Through the observation of advanced students and experts, as well as through coaching and scaffolding from a teacher, the students acquire the competences to manage complex tasks.

Implications for the use of wikis: a wiki can promote the social process of knowledge construction. Learners have to cooperate on joint work with the text in a wiki. With the use of a wiki, they have access to the knowledge of the entire community. Regardless of the presence of others, the knowledge of a community can be retrieved, which helps to solve problems that go beyond individuals' abilities, and thus enables learners to better understand their environment. This turns a wiki into a learning community where knowledge can be constructed together with others. The openness and flexibility of a wiki offers the possibility to contribute one's own knowledge to the community and find a point of contact for one's own knowledge in a wiki. The participants of a community can help new members to become a part of the learning community. A new member may at first, for example, only correct obvious spelling errors or participate only by reading. Gradually new participants will be allowed to write new text, and will grow slowly within the community in this manner. A learning community must be created around the wiki, in which the social process of knowledge construction takes place and individual learning is encouraged. For this reason, learning with wikis addresses both the development of individual knowledge as well as the development of knowledge at the community level.

INTEGRATIVE APPROACH:
KNOWLEDGE CONSTRUCTION AS A COEVOLUTION

Theoretical approach: Luhmann's (1995) theory focuses on systems and their dynamics. Systems are differentiated by their distinctive modes of operation. The mode of operation of a social system is communication. A system is also self-referential, which means it is related to itself. It understands its environment on the basis of past operations. As such, a system produces those components on its own which it needs in order to function properly. Luhmann calls this feature "autopoiesis." Systems only exist because they operate while connecting to other operations, and so a system is constantly evolving. The communication of a social system is apparently related to the environment, which the system ultimately refers to through its own perception or image of the environment. From the perspective of the system, the environment is always more complex and chaotic than the system itself.

Cress and Kimmerle (2008) apply Luhmann's system theory to knowledge construction with wikis and integrate their constructivist view. They make a distinction between two systems: the *information space* with the contents of the wiki and its associated community; and the *knowledge space* of a person's knowledge. The knowledge space contains all cognitive schemata of a person, while in the information space different kinds of information are structured and stored, such as texts, data, images, and videos. Relevant to knowledge construction are the exchange processes taking place between the knowledge space of a person and the information space of a wiki. Cress and Kimmerle propose two exchange processes between these two systems: the externalization of knowledge from the knowledge space of a person into the information space of the wiki; and the internalization of information from the information space of the wiki into the knowledge space of a person. During the externalization process, a wiki article on a certain topic is supplemented and modified with a person's knowledge. At the same time, the externalization of one's knowledge requires a deep processing and examination of the person's existing knowledge structures, and a person learns through this process. During the internalization process of the wiki information, the information present in the wiki is processed and integrated into one's knowledge structures. This results in the creation of new knowledge units and linkages among existing knowledge units in the knowledge space, and a person also learns through this process. The processes of externalization and internalization of knowledge can be described as the coevolution of knowledge space and information space. Both systems influence each other and coevolve.

Implications for the use of wikis: a wiki should be understood as a social system as defined by Luhmann. It contains the externalized knowledge of the community members as an information space. The operation mode of a wiki is written communication, which allows exchanges within the environment. The user of a wiki must adapt to the mode of operation in order to become part of the system. New information is always understood in light of the existing information in the wiki, and the already existing content in the wiki decides on the inclusion of new content. From a systemic perspective, the relevant point is the boundary between the two systems: the information space of the wiki and the knowledge space of a person. The externalization of knowledge into the wiki and the internalization of information into the knowledge space of a person takes place here. Knowledge construction with wikis must be understood as a dynamic process, in which the knowledge of individual learners and the content of a wiki mutually influence each other and coevolve. As such, reading the content in a wiki (internalization) and actively contributing content (externalization) both lead to individual learning.

MOTIVATION AND INTEREST

In addition to a description of the cognitive and social aspects of learning, as well as the attempt to describe knowledge construction with wikis from a systemic perspective, the motivational aspects of learning should also be addressed at the end of this chapter. In particular, intrinsic motivation and interest in the educational content are key factors for the success of knowledge construction. Although the influence of both factors within the school curriculum is only limited, it is worth taking a look at theoretical approaches to motivation and their implications for the use of wikis.

Theoretical approach: "intrinsic motivation" can be described as a self-desire to seek out new things. Ryan and Deci (2000) suggest three basic needs as the basis of motivation: the need for relatedness, the need for competence, and the need for autonomy. People have a basic need to feel part of a community and to be socially integrated. Self-efficacy plays an important role here, as they want to feel able and effective at influencing their own environment. They also want to be able to act and react autonomously and independently. If these three needs are satisfied, people will be intrinsically motivated. The focus of intrinsic motivation is the subject-specific interest in the learning content (Krapp, 2005). If a person considers a topic relevant and interesting, he or she will work on it more intensively. Whether learners feel self-determined, competent, and socially bound during their learning process will also depend on the topic selected by the teacher.

Implications for the use of wikis: students who are intrinsically motivated are regular and active participants in wiki communities. For this purpose, a self-determined participation is an important prerequisite. Sufficient freedom and flexibility when working with wikis are necessary to convince the learners that their own knowledge is relevant for the other participants. Even when there are certain limits set by the curriculum, being open to the interests of the learners can arouse their intrinsic motivation toward other topics. If learners can select the topics they work on or introduce their own extracurricular experiences, their interest to participate will increase. Openness to the outside environment, such as allowing other interested parties to have access to the wiki, can also enhance the students' motivation (see the chapter by Sandra Hofhues and Katharina Uhl). The challenge is to allow self-determined involvement and freedom to select personal topics in the wiki, despite the fixed performance requirements in a classroom.

CONCLUSION

This chapter gives an overview of theoretical approaches that describe knowledge construction with wikis. I have tried to draw concrete implications for the use of wikis in the classroom from these theoretical approaches. Wikis enable the emergence of cognitive conflicts and provide a platform where these conflicts can become apparent and also be solved. The community, which exists around the wiki (such as a school class), can work on the content in a collaborative manner, and the social process of knowledge construction is essentially encouraged. Finally, knowledge construction with wikis is a dynamic process. The knowledge of learners and the content of a wiki influence each other. Individual students' self-determination and their interest in the content will have a positive impact on their motivation to participate.

The theoretical considerations presented can build a bridge to concrete didactic concepts for the use of wikis. Psychological, educational, and sociological theories enhance the awareness for the potential of wikis in the classroom. As a result, there is a change in the meaning of teaching materials, as well as the role of teachers and students in the learning process. Learning becomes an active process of collaborative knowledge construction and is embedded in a knowledge community.

NOTE

1. This chapter is a shortened and revised version of Moskaliuk's book chapter (2008).

REFERENCES

Bartlett, Frederic. 1932. *Remembering.* Cambridge, UK: Cambridge University Press.

Collins, A., J. Brown, and S. Newman. 1989. "Cognitive Apprenticeship: Teaching the Crafts of Reading, Writing, and Mathematics." In *Knowing, Learning, and Instruction: Essays in Honor of Robert Glaser,* ed. L. B. Resnick, 453–94. Hillsdale, MI: Lawrence Erlbaum Associates.

Cress, U., and J. Kimmerle. 2008. "A Systemic and Cognitive View on Collaborative Knowledge Building with Wikis." *International Journal of Computer-Supported Collaborative Learning* 3, no. 2: 105–22.

Krapp, A. 2005. "Basic Needs and the Development of Interest and Intrinsic Motivational Orientations." *Learning and Instruction* 15, no. 5: 381–95.

Luhmann, N. 1995. *Social Systems.* Stanford, CA: Stanford University Press.

Moskaliuk, J. 2008. "Wissenskonstruktion mit Wikis aus konstruktivistischer und systemtheoretischer Sicht." In *Konstruktion und Kommunikation von Wissen mit Wikis,* ed. J. Moskaliuk, 51–68. Boizenburg: Verlag Werner Hülsbusch.

Piaget, J. 1977. *The Development of Thought: Equilibration of Cognitive Structures.* New York: Viking.

Rumelhart, D. 1980. "Schemata: The Building Blocks of Cognition." In *Theoretical Issues in Reading Comprehension,* ed. R. J. Spiro, 33–58. Hillsdale, NJ: Lawrence Erlbaum Associates.

Ryan, R. M., and E. L. Deci. 2000. "Self-Determination Theory and the Facilitation of Intrinsic Motivation, Social Development, and Well-Being." *American Psychologist* 55, no. 1: 68–78.

Scardamalia, M., and C. Bereiter. 2006. "Knowledge Building: Theory, Pedagogy, and Technology." In *The Cambridge Handbook of the Learning Sciences,* ed. K. Sawyer, 97–115. New York: Cambridge University Press.

Vygotsky, L. S. 1986. *Denken und Sprechen.* Frankfurt: Fischer Taschenbuch-Verlag.

SANDRA HOFHUES
AND KATHARINA UHL

3

Learning in the Field of Tension between Public Opening and Openness

SCHOOLS AND THE PUBLIC: A (SHORT) REVIEW

Schools are public institutions. They are perceived as an educational environment, an entity for meditation and reflection, a protected learning space, and are associated with a sociocultural stage of life. This diverse picture of a school manifests itself in its education mandates on the one hand, and is also shaped by the people in the school, in terms of their perception of their school and how they present it to a dispersed (i.e., completely unknown [Maletzke, 1998]) educational or personal public body on the other. At the same time, schools are institutions of public interest, and discussions about the results, values, and relationships in the school (Schein, 1980) are likely to be experienced by each teacher, every day. It is also likely that the self-image of the school does not conform to its public image. On the contrary, the self-image and public image of the school may often drift apart.

The self-image of the school expresses itself in the documents regarding its structure and organization, as well as in the school environment (Fend, 2001, 81ff.). Two representative studies from the Allensbach Institute (IfD, 2010; Köcher, 2009) based on face-to-face interviews offer an insight into the public image of the school. From an external perspective, both studies point out that

- The expectations for the educational context of the school are complex.
- Public expectations are mixed with the internal school experiences (e.g., through the parents).
- The school is held responsible for individual student performance, without involving the learning conditions of the student in detail.

For the teachers, it is specifically expected that a variety of teaching methodologies are used. A variation in learning features could also imply the hope of opening-up the lessons. Poor teaching and a lack of teaching commitment can lead to public complaints against the school and against specific lessons (IfD, 2010, 14; Köcher, 2009, 18). Although studies about school images and teacher profiles are frequently criticized for their quantitative approach, Oelkers (2009, 63ff.) has summarized in his re-analysis that teachers are often publicly perceived as "indifferent, with too little engagement" (Ibid., 65). However, as he has already pointed out in an earlier publication, it is up to the schools to determine "the change of their product" from the inside out (Oelkers, 2003, 55).

Corresponding to the context of this chapter, it will be interesting to see how schools *can* counteract the (occasional) bad school image, and also whether schools *want* to be in favor of pedagogic-didactic innovations, because typically it is the latter and not the public image of the school that convinces the school management to implement new features together with those involved in everyday teaching. These new features can certainly become a media-based tool in their character, since digital media can specifically reach the targeted educational public (i.e., stakeholders). Very often, such pedagogical innovations began with a change of teaching in terms of the internal school development (Hofhues, 2011, 179ff.).

LEARNING AMONG PUBLIC PERCEPTIONS, THE OPENING-UP PROCESS, AND AN OPEN ATTITUDE

It has previously been stated that the opening-up of the school and lessons can have a positive effect on the public image of the school. However, the public image of the school is rarely influenced by learning in a public environment. Rather, the public is helpful in creating an authentic and well-situated learning environment for schools in a formal educational context. In other words, the public helps to facilitate learning based on everyday situations, or at least provides an anchor for the processing of everyday experiences. It should be noted that the ubiquity of computers, the Internet, and digital media belongs permanently to everyday (media) life. Technological developments also blur the boundaries between public and private spheres, and the thematization of their content in schools is educationally necessary. One can specifically make use of publicness from the point of view of pedagogic-didactical interests, in order to experience the dynamics of media activity in a protected school space and to reflect on them.

In view of the conception and implementation of public teaching-learning settings, the conceptual differences between "publicness," "opening-up," and "openness" should be differentiated. These three terms have their origins in different disciplines, and as a consequence, they address different components of the *public*. In addition, they set different temporal markers: while some disciplines consider publicness as an already achieved status, others find the shaping process of publicness under the aspect of social participation particularly significant.

According to Habermas (1981a, 1981b), in sociology and communication science, *publicness* is an essential part of the opinion-forming process. Publicness plays a part in the fact that opinions are medially conveyed, whereby the opinion formation of the public is initiated. During this conveying process, publicness fulfils its transparency, validation, and orientation functions (Neidhardt, 1994). Publicness enables access to information, supports discussions, and generates opinions through interpersonal exchanges. Moreover, in addition to thematization strategies, persuasion strategies can be applicable in situations of public communication, in order to enforce opinions normatively. The validation function of publicness also sets the biggest value for the teaching-learning context. Students and teachers can learn how to deal with topics, and to form and exchange their opinions. They can also orient themselves and the effect of their learning process on them (Hofhues, 2010; 2011). A sociologist would mainly look at publicness as a status that has already been achieved. Questions regarding the constitution of publicness would primarily be considered on the basis of its medial effects, and are less likely to be looked at under the aspect of the pedagogic-didactic structuring of knowledge, learning, and education. Instead, this notion is often perceived as participation or enlightenment and as an educational goal (e.g., Oelkers, 1992).

Besides public opinion (see above), Wilbers (2004) points out that three additional components of publicness can be distinguished. They are related to sociology, but are rather characterized in terms of the sociology of organizations, and less as an aspect of communication science. These three components are (1) the regulatory public that determines the organization of the school; (2) the public with control of educational policies, that decides and distributes the curricular content; and (3) a critical public that results from the technical work with the educational context of the school. All three components of the public are relevant to the school, since they determine both the abstract and the distanced nature of the school system, as well as the critical details about an individual school and its development. People remain largely invisible, unless they make themselves seen by giving individual or collaborative opinions. The latter represents a challenge for the schools' public relations and professional manner (Oelkers, 2009, 82).

Because public relations are created by relationships between people and their interactions, this means that the image of a school as represented in the public may not correspond to the locally shaped external perception of that individual school. If the public sees teaching and learning as a didactic tool, the positive and negative aspects of the shaping of external perceptions should be considered. This innovation is more related to the challenges of the local individual school and less to the school image. However, good and bad examples in the implementation can be turned into concrete reasons for discussing an individual school in this manner, and can also be personally related under certain circumstances.

In addition to *publicness,* the concept of *opening-up exists.* The opening-up of schools and lessons is proclaimed as an increasing orientation for action and resolving problems, as a result of didactic principles (Hallitzky and Seibert, 2002, 169). At the same time, transparent processes and efforts of opening-up are considered an indication of a good school (Fend, 2001), and they play a significant role in school development processes. In contrast to the concept of publicness, opening-up is to be understood here as a movement of internal school stakeholders, as opposed to external people, organizations, or innovations. It is therefore meant to be a deliberate transformation or process aimed at making changes to the school and lessons, by creating disturbances of the normal school routines. The nature of the process is both an opportunity and an obstacle. The opening up of a school incorporates the basic ideas of many approaches to school development, but at the same time due to its own dynamics, such openings are difficult to be planned. This difficulty to plan also means that the teachers often shy away from the opening-up processes. The challenges of opening-up can be limiting (e.g., support of a self-organized teaching-learning process, dealing with criticism, etc.), but their positive and negative effects cannot be planned.

Unlike the concept of publicness, the term *opening-up* is consistently found in pedagogical-didactic literature. Opening-up is proclaimed as a didactic principle for modernizing schools and learning, in the hope to change teaching and learning styles. Very often, a marginal point is omitted from the concepts, which is the necessary openness of learners and teachers to move to the open learning environment and deal with open teaching-learning settings. This requirement may sound trivial, but it is highly significant for the technical content and the socio-communicative design of the learning process. As an example, it should be noted that even the German Education Council demanded openness as a necessary sociocultural attitude for teachers, in order to create a transition between school and later occupations. Openness represents permeability, dynamics, and flexibility (Risse, 2003, 48). Open-mindedness can overcome limits, and is often associated with closedness. However, closedness is not necessarily counterproductive or dysfunctional. On the contrary, closed structures can provide a solid orientation and stability in a school, especially for less experienced learners (Hallitzky and Seibert, 2002, 172).

Pedagogical-didactic considerations basically assume the compatibility of the aforementioned terms and concepts. Learning content, however, also becomes a focus in the area of openness. After all, the consideration of implementing wikis in schools, which is characterized by the core principle of openness, has resulted in the "juggling" of many concepts and terms. While openness as an attitude has previously been discussed, openness as a wiki principle will be given special attention in the following section.

OPENNESS AS A WIKI PRINCIPLE

It is not without reason that one connects openness as a central principle for the use of a wiki. Wikis are technically and culturally open in their fundamental basis. After Cunningham launched his original version of a wiki, everyone could access the wiki and change its content and structure (Döbeli Honegger, 2005; 2006; Ebersbach, Glaser, and Heigl, 2008). Open wikis are available under the regulations of the GNU Free Documentation License, which stipulates that texts may be used as long as their source is provided with a link. Other hurdles allow for ease of access, as well as further processing and distribution. From a user perspective, wikis are established based on an open-minded attitude and a low hierarchical structure. The latter personal openness allows collective intelligence, which could, with the wiki principle, become the "wisdom of crowds" (e.g., Grant, 2006).

Even though openness is described as a characteristic wiki principle and forms the basis of self-organized work, not every wiki is publicly accessible (Döbeli Honegger, 2006; Moskaliuk, 2008). Strictly speaking, the majority of wikis implemented in school classrooms are closed (i.e., they are internal systems for use in the lessons). The teachers have the possibility to make the writing process or its results accessible on the World Wide Web, the school Intranet, or on local computers, as well as to distinguish between read and write permissions. Openness may also mean the disclosure of the identity of the participants. The question of how much publicness versus how much privacy should be involved is discussed under the heading of "personal public-ness," which also leads to the question of whether students should use their real names and be thereby identifiable, or should use arbitrary names when using digital media like wikis (e.g., Schmidt, 2008, 32ff.). Structurally, there can be different degrees of openness, depending on the teacher's didactic point of view and the teaching-learning scenario. Closed wikis are likely to be predominantly used in instructional scenarios, while fully open wikis are best fitted to scenarios with a higher amount of construction activities (see more detail in Reinmann and Mandl, 2006). However, these are just rough bound-aries, and the different ways of usage are quite well-mixed in school practice. As to the question of whether a closed new wiki or work on an existing wiki should be preferred (Moskaliuk, 2008, 6), the answer will depend on each individual case. Whether the wikis are used independently or are externally controlled will also depend on the didactic scenarios. Before the implemen-tation of a wiki, the teacher needs to specify a degree of openness, and many so-called hybrid forms come about in schools that are in the middle of the continuum and that connect instruction with construction.

If teachers decide to use a wiki, they often prefer *closed wikis*. These allow students to engage with one another within a medial protected space, in which learners and teachers can try out various aspects of the wiki. Similarly, they offer teachers the opportunity to embed the use of media in current teach-ing activities and to make these part of an examination. In closed scenarios, access to the wikis remains reserved for the particular group. Its structure can be determined by the teacher beforehand, and students can do their school-work more easily in the wiki, or with the help of the wiki. It is also possible to incorporate the wiki as a standard testing format, because the user identity is clear in the wiki. One can do homework or write further texts with the help of the wiki. The difference is that students can work collaboratively and the learning progress of individuals and groups can be demonstrated on the basis of version history. At the same time, access should be protected to prevent vandalism (Ebersbach, Glaser, and Heigl, 2008; Döbeli Honegger, 2006).

If closed wikis are used in the lessons, their potential as teaching-learning tools can be developed, in the sense that they support students in gathering and preparing learning materials, which then can be shared and assessed in class. The number of users is limited. Only when the teachers gradually open up their lessons, allowing for interaction in the wiki with people outside the classroom, will greater potentials become feasible (for example, an internal opening-up within the school), which could lead to cooperation with another class or an interaction with specialists. Just imagine such an opening-up where experts from politics, business, and science could be involved in this teaching-learning process. However, these people would require access to the platform and the authorization to read and edit student work if they are to participate with the class. Their access could be occasional or permanent, and their possibilities of action determined by the teacher. These people outside the classroom are then specifically integrated into the classroom, and have certain rights to fulfill specific tasks.

On a closer examination of the topic, no principled position on the openness or closedness of Wikis can be taken. Instead, when deciding to employ or not to employ a public wiki, it is also important to examine carefully the lesson content and objectives, as well as the target group. The reason is that although wikis require little experience in their technical usage, ways to cope with public interactions have to be learned (Konieczny, 2007). For inexperienced users, it is expected to be a euphoric but not a profoundly critical media activity. In general, public learning situations can overwhelm the learners. Some basic pedagogical-didactic questions regarding the opening-up of lessons are associated with the planning of public wikis. Planning should include, for example, reflection on the objectives of the use of the wiki, the students' experience, the learning context and objectives, the teaching methods and the general learning organization (Kerres, 2001). Especially with regard to the learning organization, challenges can arise in terms of learning support, and depending on the scenario, organizational, content, personal, and technical matters can be involved (de Witt, 2005). It is also true that, while maintaining openness as an attitude, unplanned challenges from the use of media should be expected (Grant, 2006).

However, *all* contradictions that are inherent in the scenarios cannot be solved; if one decides on a criterion for the use of the wiki, one is deciding against other opposite criteria at the same time. This means that wikis which are open and accessible for all cannot be closed wikis (i.e., only accessible to a limited number of users at the same time). Inexperienced users cannot become experienced after using wikis for only a short time (e.g., in one lesson hour). The voluntary nature of this learning activity is also limited by the associated tests and examinations. Informal learning is subject to planned limits by its integration in a formal education context.

POTENTIALS AND CHALLENGES OF IMPLEMENTING WIKIS IN PUBLIC TEACHING-LEARNING SETTINGS

The use of wikis in formal educational contexts, such as in a school, is often associated with the hope to achieve development in teaching and the school through the use of media and pedagogical-didactic innovations. Specifically, the practical orientation is considered an opportunity for learning as such, and is an emancipatory idea for education. The learners become more involved in learning than before, and their change in learning behavior is recognized. Students are often fascinated, irritated, or "eager to be surprised" by the possibilities of media use (Forte and Bruckman, 2009). Teachers, however, are often less enthusiastic about the technical opportunities to deepen or change the way of teaching brought about by the use of wikis. Above all, they are concerned with safeguarding all personal rights when developing media-based didactic scenarios, in which active media activities are possible and can be considered critical and thought-provoking in a protected area.

As a result, no blueprint can be formulated for how wikis shall be used in the classroom. Rather, it can be said that open teaching-learning settings, as a general rule, have a motivating effect on the learners. It is personally significant for them when they can present their learning context to a group of people publicly (e.g., on the Internet), and this in turn increases their self-efficacy, which is of paramount importance for intrinsic motivation in learning (Deci and Ryan, 1993; Reinmann and Bianco, 2008). The authentic learning context can also help students to understand, for example, the use of the wiki, the basic principles of knowledge sharing in Web 2.0, and to develop an open attitude. Furthermore, wiki-work in public often has an effect on the quality of a presentation and the ability for its critical evaluation, which allows the participants to develop their media and information literacy (Pelka, 2007; Schiefner-Rohs, 2012). It has been shown, for example, that students are not used to assessing the work of their classmates: they think the modification of others' wiki texts is a rude behavior, with the exception of small linguistic corrections. It is necessary for them to get used to handling criticism (Grant, 2006; Konieczny, 2007). Another equally critical issue is that when students examine the changes made in their own content, they also consider this a kind of intervention in another's work (ibid.). However, this represents a learning opportunity for the students arising from the use of media as a source, and media as the place of presentation (or criticism). The students learn to do research, to coordinate in the group, to present the information, and to deal with feedback. In addition, the risk of plagiarism is reduced, as contents are accessible to teachers and also among the students themselves.

Despite the doubts about their authenticity as a learning activity, closed wikis are generally assumed to be better for students and learners. Students will feel less (public) pressure to achieve results, or to be observed by classmates and outsiders. Whether personal learning achievements, with all the associated effects of using a public, open wiki, can be greater than using a non-public, closed wiki, depends on the learning objective and context and must be assessed on a case-by-case basis. From other contexts (e.g., universities), it is known that openness of media use is a necessary prerequisite for lively participation, but on the other hand, such openness in use can sometimes lead to smaller participation (Grell and Rau, 2008). However, there are probably more sustainable learning experiences as a result of the opening-up process, which make an important contribution to the deepening of learned knowledge and ultimately to individual learning success.

Finally, it should be specified that for the implementation of a wiki in school, there are less public wikis that can help to develop or further develop the school's media tools. Indeed, an open attitude of the teachers as well as the students is considered important, or even the most important element to school development, because such an attitude entails both external effects (e.g., signs of transparency) and internal effects (e.g., authentic and well-positioned teaching-learning settings). To make an informed decision about the use of wikis, teachers should, above all, give it due pedagogical-didactic considerations and not be guided or misled by technical opportunities, because the use of wikis is dependent on the content to be taught, as well as the target groups that will use (or should use) the digital media. In addition, framework conditions such as support configurations or examination formats must be considered, as well as the requirements of the teacher. How will the implementation of the wiki be carried out in the school? How can innovative teachers, without technical knowledge, strive to integrate wikis (or other digital media) into their lessons, supported by school administration and staff (e.g., Herzig and Grafe, 2010)? Wiki use in schools affects not only the micro-didactic level of lessons and media usage scenarios, on which the accessibility of wikis has been discussed, but is also always embedded in a more extended reflection on the theme of a "good school," which was mentioned at the beginning of this chapter and remains open for discussion.

REFERENCES

Deci, E., and R. Ryan. 1993. "Die Selbstbestimmungstheorie der Motivation und ihre Bedeutung für die Pädagogik." *Zeitschrift für Pädagogik* 2: 223–38.

Deutscher, Bildungsrat. 1974. *Zur Neuordnung der Sekundarstufe II: Konzept für eine Verbindung von allgemeinem und beruflichem Lernen.* Stuttgart: Klett.

de Witt, C. 2005. "E-Learning." In *Grundbegriffe Medienpädagogik,* ed. J. Hüther and B. Schorb. 74–81. 4th edition. Munich: kopaed.

Döbeli Honegger, B. 2005. "Wiki und die starken Lehrerinnen." In *Unterrichtskonzepte für informatische Bildung,* ed. S. Friedrich, 173–83. Lecture Notes in Informatics.

———. 2006. "Wiki und die starken Texte: Schreibprojekte mit Wikis." *Deutschmagazin* 1: 15–19.

Ebersbach, A., M. Glaser, and R. Heigl. 2008. *Social Web.* Konstanz: UVK.

Fend, H., and Verlagsgesellschaft. 2001. *Qualität im Bildungswesen: Schulforschung zu Systembedingungen, Schulprofilen und Lehrerleistung.* 2nd edition. Weinheim: Juventa-Verlag.

Forte, A., and A. Bruckman. 2009. "Writing, Citing, and Participatory Media: Wikis as Learning Environments in the High School Classroom." *International Journal of Learning and Media* 4, no. 1: 23–44.

Grant, L. 2006. "Using Wikis in Schools: A Case Study." http://rhazen.edublogs .org/files/2008/01/wikis_in_schools_futurelab.pdf.

Grell, P., and F. Rau. 2008. "Partizipationslücken—Social Software in der Hochschullehre." *Medienpädagogik* 21: 1–23.

Habermas, J. 1981a. *Theorie des kommunikativen Handelns: Handlungsrationalität und gesellschaftliche Rationalisierung.* Volume 1. Frankfurt: Suhrkamp.

———. 1981b. *Theorie des kommunikativen Handelns: Zur Kritik der funktionalistischen Vernunft.* Volume 2. Frankfurt: Suhrkamp.

Hallitzky, M., and N. Seibert. 2002. "Theorie des Unterrichts: Von bildungs-theoretischen zu systemtheoretisch-konstruktivistischen Ansätzen in der Didaktik." In *Studienbuch Schulpädagogik,* ed. H. J. Apel and W. Sacher, 133–80. Bad Heilbrunn: Klinkhardt.

Herzig, B., and S. Grafe. 2010. "Digitale Lernwelten und Schule." In *Digitale Lernwelten: Konzepte, Beispiele und Perspektiven,* ed. K.-U. Hugger and M. Walber, 115–27. Wiesbaden: VS.

Hofhues, S. 2010. "Die Rolle von Öffentlichkeit im Lehr-Lernprozess." In *Digitale Medien für Lehre und Forschung,* ed. S. Mandel, M. Rutishauser, and E. Seiler Schiedt, 405–14. Reihe Medien in der Wissenschaft, vol. 55. Münster: Waxmann.

———. 2011. *Lernen durch Kooperation: Potenziale der Zusammenarbeit von Schulen und Unternehmen am Beispiel eines Schule-Wirtschaft-Projekts.* Dissertation. Munich: Universität der Bundeswehr, Fakultät für Pädagogik.

IfD (Institut für Demoskopie Allensbach). 2010. "Aktuelle Fragen der Schulpolitik und das Bild der Lehrer in Deutschland. Eine Studie des Instituts für Demoskopie Allensbach im Auftrag der Vodafone Stiftung Deutschland." **www.lehrerpreis.de/documents/Digitale_Pressemappe.pdf.**

Kerres, M. 2001. "Online- und Präsenzelemente in hybriden Lernarrangements kombinieren." In *Handbuch E-Learning,* ed. A. Hohenstein and K. Wilbers, 1–9. Cologne: Fachverlag Deutscher Wirtschaftsdienst.

Köcher, R. 2009. "Schulen und Lehrer aus Sicht der Bevölkerung: Unterricht innovativ–Deutscher Lehrpreis." www.vodafone-stiftung.de/upload/pdf/ IfD_Allensbach.pdf.

Konieczny, P. 2007. "Wikis and Wikipedia as a Teaching Tool." *International Journal of Instructional Technology and Distance Learning* 4, no. 1: 16–34.

Maletzke, G. 1998. *Kommunikationswissenschaft im Überblick.* Wiesbaden: VS Verlag für Sozialwissenschaften.

Moskaliuk, J. 2008. "Das Wiki-Prinzip." In *Konstruktion und Kommunikation von Wissen mit Wikis: Theorie und Praxis*, ed. J. Moskaliuk, 17–27. Boizenburg: Verlag Werner Hülsbusch.

Neidhardt, F. 1994. "Öffentlichkeit, öffentliche Meinung, soziale Bewegungen." In Öffentlichkeit, öffentliche Meinung, soziale Bewegungen, ed. F. Neidhardt. Special issue 42/2002 of *Kölner Zeitschrift für Soziologie und Sozialpsychologie*. Opladen: Westdeutscher Verlag.

Oelkers, J. 1992. "Einleitung: Aufklärung als Lernprozess." *Zeitschrift für Pädagogik* 28: 9–23. Special issue.

———. 2003. "Schulen in erweiterter Verantwortung. Eine Positionsbestimmung aus e ziehungswissenschaftlicher Sicht." In *Zur Modernisierung der Schule: Leitideen—Konzepte—Akteure. Ein Überblick*, ed. T. Brüsemeister and K.-D. Eubel, 54–63. Bielefeld: transcript Verlag.

———. 2009. "'I Wanted to Be a Good Teacher . . . .' Zur Ausbildung von Lehrkräften in Deutschland: Netzwerk Bildung." Berlin: FES.

Pelka, B. 2007. *Das Prinzip Wiki in der Praxis: Theorie, Anwendung, Anleitung*. Hannover: Institut für Journalistik und Kommunikationsforschung (IJK).

Reinmann, G., and T. Bianco. 2008. *Knowledge Blogs zwischen Kompetenz, Autonomie und sozialer Eingebundenheit* (Arbeitsbericht no. 17). Augsburg: Universität Augsburg.

Reinmann, G., and H. Mandl. 2006. "Unterrichten und Lernumgebungen gestalten." In *Pädagogische Psychologie: Ein Lehrbuch, 5, vollständig überarbeitete Auflage*, ed. A. Krapp and B. Weidenmann, 613–58. Weinheim: BeltzPVU.

Risse, E. 2003. *Lernkultur als Ziel einer systemischen Entwicklung der Schule*. Oldenburger Universitätsreden no. 145. Oldenburg: Bibliotheks- und Informationssystem der Universität Oldenburg.

Schein, E. H. 1980. *Organisationspsychologie*. Wiesbaden: Gabler Verlag.

Schiefner-Rohs, M. 2012. *Kritische Informations- und Medienkompetenz: Theoretisch-konzeptionelle Herleitung und empirische Betrachtungen am Beispiel der Lehrerausbildung*. Dissertation, Internationale Hochschulschriften. Münster: Waxmann.

Schmidt, J. 2008. "Was ist neu am Social Web? Soziologische und kommunika-tionswissen-schaftliche Grundlagen." In *Kommunikation, Partizipation und Wirkungen im Social Web, vol. 1: Grundlagen und Methoden: Von der Gesellschaft zum Individuum*, ed. A. Zerfass, M. Welker, and J. Schmidt, 18–40. Cologne: Herbert von Halem Verlag.

Wilbers, K. 2004. *Soziale Netzwerke an berufsbildenden Schulen: Analyse, Potentiale, Gesta tungsansätze*. Paderborn: Eusl-Verlag.

MICHELE NOTARI AND
BEAT DÖBELI HONEGGER

4
How to Collaborate Using a Wiki

THIS CHAPTER SHOWS THE POTENTIAL OF A WIKI ENGINE TO perform collaboration within a learning scenario. It starts with an explanation of why collaboration has to be scaffolded and what specific tools within a wiki enhance collaboration among learners. The chapter ends with an example of a concrete learning scenario applying the mentioned methods and techniques.

WHY IS IT USEFUL TO STRUCTURE COLLABORATION?

Collaborative learning is not always effective; its effects depend on the richness and intensity of interactions engaged by group members during collaboration (Dillenbourg, 1999). Learning outcomes are related to the emergence of elaborated explanations, the negotiation of meanings, the quality of argumentation structures, and the mutual regulation of cognitive processes. Following Dillenbourg and Hong (2008), many approaches exist by means of which a computer-supported collaborative learning (CSCL) environment can directly or indirectly shape group interactions, namely:

"By designing a communication tool, for instance semi-structured interfaces, that proposes predefined speech acts in the form of buttons or sentence openers" (Baker and Lund, 1996; Veerman and Treasure-Jones, 1999; Soller, 2001). "By shaping (graphical) representations of the task and the objects to be manipulated by students (Suthers, 1999).

"By forming groups in a specific way"; "By providing team members with a representation of their interactions in order to foster regulation at the group level" (Dillenbourg et al., 2002; Jermann and Dillenbourg, 2008); "By providing feedback on the quality of group interactions." See also various similar approaches as reviewed by Jermann et al. (2001); "By scripting the collaboration process using specific phases, roles and activities" (Weinberger et al., 2002; Dillenbourg and Hong, 2008).

In addition to proposing tools for optimizing pivotal moments of collaboration planning and scaffolding, the *design* of lessons is crucial for optimal collaboration.

INQUIRY-BASED LEARNING MODEL AND ABAHCOCOSUCOL AS A METHOD FOR EFFECTIVE COLLABORATION IN A TECHNOLOGY-ENHANCED LEARNING SETTING

Scaffolding the curriculum enhances effectiveness of collaboration. The following section shows two examples of storyboards focusing on feedback culture, phasing different didactical activities, and other interventions for optimizing collaboration.

Action Based, Hypertext—Constructive, Computer-Supported, Collaborative Learning Model (ABAHCOCOSUCOL)

This model is meant to be used in formal learning settings. Target audiences include high school or university students. The model has not been used for K-8 education (Notari, 2003). Scripting for ABAHCOCOSUCOL can be cut into four phases: creating content using a hypertext, linking concepts, comparing and peer-commenting, and regrouping concepts within the hypertext. An initiation phase leads students into the problem and gives them an indication for an appropriate first action. For this phase, there is no big difference between an ABAHCOCOSUCOL and "conventional" teaching. Learners get an introduction into the subject by the teacher and start creating, individually or in small groups, hypertext-content. It is crucial to create enough content (called "critical mass of input") in a first learning phase.

The comparison phase should start immediately after a critical mass of input has been created. Within the comparison phase learners are invited to read the work of their peers and then to find and link similarities within the created content. The learners can compare immediately and simultaneously the content created by their peers. Such a comparison of ongoing work within a learning community is difficult to realize in a traditional (non-computer-supported) curriculum. Being aware of all other inputs of the community, a single learner can compare the quality of his or her contribution with other contributions, and gets a formative evaluation about his or her work. Commenting on other tasks enhances social competences and meta-cognitive skills. The comparison phase then leads into the regrouping of the work produced, which aids in the construction of mental models of the different concepts and is fruitful for learning. This sets the stage for the discussion phase, and the feedback and comment culture described above leads to a regrouping of the content.

These phases can be repeated more than once. At the end of the learning unit a discussion should give students the opportunity to formulate and discuss different opinions or concepts. The positive feedback cycle of production, comparison, and regrouping can also be formulated in the following way as noted in figure 4.1.

Scripting should induce students to publish what they have produced as soon as possible, and it should be mentioned that there will be an "evolution" of the content during the unit due to the comments and questions of the other members of the community. The "critical mass" of input at the beginning is important for the start of interactions among learners and the creation of a communication culture. Of course, other "creating inputs" can be made during the learning unit; for instance, when new questions arise.

The linking of concepts is important for student understanding of the common goal and the cross-linkage of the concepts of the unit treated. The learning community creates one collaboratively elaborated hypertext where the different pages are interwoven and linked. Creating links sustains the awareness of the community and gives a basis for the comments and comparisons produced as a further action of the students. Finally, the distillation and

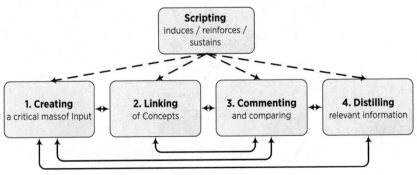

FIGURE 4.1
ABAHCOCOSUCOL model (Notari, 2006).

regrouping of relevant information leads to a self-evaluation of the product in the learning community.

The principal settings of ABAHCOCOSUCOL can be used for a large range of educational purposes. They are not bound to a specific school subject or to a learning environment where students and teachers see each other regularly. The major advantages of the model are the quick setup when the model is applied using a wiki, and the considerable adaptability and the scalability of the system. ABAHCOCOSUCOL has been adapted for high school students in different non-experimental learning settings and in a blended distance education course about media methodology with adults.

Using ABAHCOCOSUCOL showed good learning performances concerning the following competences and skills: increase of factual knowledge, long-term knowledge retention, development of problem-solving strategies, ability to construct a hypertext, linking concepts and distilling relevant information to regroup concepts, and increased metacognitive skills (Notari, 2003).

Progressive Inquiry Model

In a progressive inquiry process (Hakkarainen and Sintonen, 2002; Muukkonen, Lakkala, and Hakkarainen, 2008), the teacher creates a context for

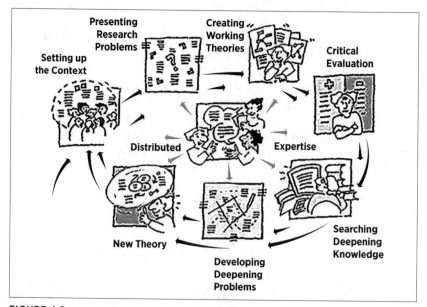

FIGURE 4.2

Progressive inquiry model (Hakkarainen and Sintonen, 2002; Muukkonen, Lakkala, and Hakkarainen, 2008, 22).

inquiry by presenting a multidisciplinary approach to a theoretical or real-life phenomenon, after which the students start defining their own questions. Students' questions and explanations are shared and evaluated together, which directs the utilization of authoritative information sources and iterative elaboration of subordinate study questions and more advanced theories, explanations, and writings. The model is not meant prescriptively, as an ideal path to be followed rigidly; rather, it offers conceptual tools to describe, understand, and take into account the critical elements in collaborative knowledge-advancing inquiry. (See figure 4.2.) Hakkarainen and Sintonen (2002) note that this type of inquiry separates two levels and two types of questions: "First, there are initial, principal questions determined by the goals of inquiry, and small subordinate questions that need to be answered in order to approach the principal question; second, there is a distinction between ill-defined explanation-seeking why-questions and well-defined so-called wh-questions (i.e., who-, where-, when-, and which) and yes/no questions. Principal questions are often explanation-seeking in nature, emerging from inquirers' need to understand new phenomena on the basis of their existing knowledge" (2002). Such an inquiry approach can be applied well using the wiki practices put forth above.

WIKI, A TOOL FOR ACTIVE CONSTRUCTIVE LEARNING

Wikis for Learning

Thus far we have described a theoretical model adapted to ubiquitous social and active learning in the digital age, the importance of structure within a collaboration act, and discussed two different types of strategies empowering collaborative learning. We now present an overview of the tool features and affordances that accommodate the qualities described.

Wikis are the simplest form of a web-based content management system, invented by Ward Cunningham in 1995 (Leuf and Cunningham, 2001). In the beginning they were used for informal learning. Cunningham invented them to create and collect, and then to share and discuss software patterns within the programming community. After some time, the potential of wikis to construct, create, and share concepts within a learning community by creating and building a hypertext was also discovered for use in formal learning settings both at the university (Guzdial, Rick, and Kehoe, 2001) and school levels (Notari, 2003, Désilets, Paquet, and Vinson, 2005; Desilets and Paquet, 2005; Döbeli Honegger, 2005). Here we emphasize constructive uses of wikis for learning in which students are creators, more so than such sites' non-constructivist uses as information repositories (e.g., Wikipedia) and information sources, which do not much differ from the use of traditional websites.

Key Constructivist Properties of Wikis and Their Potential to Afford Learning

In the Internet time scale the wiki concept invented in 1995 is a relatively old one. Both wikis and their contexts have evolved in the last twenty years. Nowadays many wiki properties can be found in other social media and content management system tools and settings. Nevertheless, the wiki concept is still important as a pioneering technology and an archetype for later tools, and is a platform still in use in many practical work contexts today. In the following section we present the respective properties of a wiki, which make such a platform archetypical as a learning and teaching tool for the digital age.

A wiki can be defined as:

> a web server with revision control on the internet, where everybody can easily create, change and link web pages without additional tools or knowledge of HTML. (Döbeli Honegger, 2007)

Affordances in wikis that support learning including the following components.

"Create": Creating Content

In a wiki students can easily contribute texts in a variety of multimedia forms. This affordance has several potentials: writing can be motivating when the result is visible for others (Cohen and Riel, 1989; Schrackmann et al., 2008), from their classmates to wider audiences of the World Wide Web. Writing is always an active and constructive activity. On the whole, writing can foster learning. Writing-to-learn is addressed in a family of instructional design models that postulate the positive effects of pedagogical scenarios that engage learners in writing activities (Klein, 1999; Galbraith, 1999).

"Link": Linking Content

Wikis (like every hypertext system) allow links between different parts of a text. In order to find hypertexts that can be linked, students must read and understand elements they want to link to, and identify fitting relations. This activity enhances deep understanding of the topic and allows connections to be made between student pages and pages of experts outside the formal learning setting (building in a type of informal learning as well).

"Change": Editing Content

Wikis ease the modification of content. Students can revise their own and other complex wiki texts in an easier way than in paper-based texts produced by a learning community. This can improve the quality of the end result and enhance attention to the content.

"Everybody": Collaborative Editing

Wikis ease collaborative content creation, fostering group work, openness allowing for evolving content, and direct collaboration mediated by the online environment. When two or more users try to edit the same page some wiki engines disable collaboration in order to prevent two people from changing the same text. More current wiki tools can accommodate editing conflicts by saving and refreshing almost permanently and creating many different versions of the same text in a short time. Students can also incorporate the use of GoogleDocs for real-time collaborative editing into their synchronous and asynchronous wiki editing to accommodate publication of content that requires timely but not simultaneous collaborative updating.

"Revision Control": Being Process-Aware

The revision control of wikis and the history record provided lowers the danger and damage of vandalism. Vandalism occurs more so in large unpersonalized wikis like Wikipedia than in small wikis created and supported by a niche community. Revision control can make visible the process of content generation. Learners and teachers can reconstruct how a text develops. Thinking about how a certain text evolved during the creation period is fruitful for reflecting the learning process and fosters metacognitive skills.

"On the Internet": Working in the Cloud

Because wikis can be hosted on a server on the Internet, educational institutions don't have to install hardware in their own buildings and the wiki is reachable from everywhere (Wilson, 2008). This networked model is also called "cloud computing" (Chellappa and Gupta, 2007) and eases the mobility of the learner and therefore also informal learning. Wikis work without local installed additional tools. To work on a wiki, only a web browser is needed. So there is no need for software installation on the computers of the learners and every device that can be used to surf the Web is also usable as a wiki client. This lowers the barriers for using wikis as a learning tool in various contexts.

On a higher level of abstraction, wikis can be described as open, process-oriented, and content-focused (Leuf and Cunningham, 2001; Iske and Marotzki, 2009)

"Open": Wiki Is Inviting Everybody

Wikis are open in several ways, creating an inviting character. A classic wiki has *no restrictions on reading or writing* on a wiki page. This fosters collaboration, inviting students and teachers to peruse and change or enhance content. The users in education settings have to negotiate power structures on a social level. Such interactions can lead to a more evenly distributed authority between teachers and learners (Richardson, 2006, 61). A classic wiki has *no predefined structure* and is therefore like a blank slate. Editing is simplified through the push of a submit button. The content structure has to be defined by writers themselves. This lack of structure may be inviting for some but less so for others. In a classic wiki it is possible to write the title of a placeholder wiki page as a future reference, thus inviting everybody to create this page with a single click.

"Process-Oriented": The Journey Is the Reward

In a wiki not only the result, but also the process is relevant. The revision control, the so-called RecentChanges page, and the corresponding RSS feed ease the monitoring of changes in a wiki. Theoretically, work in a wiki is never completed. Wikis are focused on further development, both enhancing and reworking existing content. This property of wikis can be used on a short-term basis as described above. It can also match certain learning scenarios on a longer time scale. Wiki also supports the didactical concept of a spiral curriculum (Bruner, 1960) where the same subject is treated different times in increasing depth.

"Content-Focused": Wikis Don't Provide Whistles and Bells

Ward Cunningham once defined a wiki as "the simplest online database that could possibly work." Because wikis do not allow sophisticated formatting and styling of web pages, the focus is on content and not on form. While the author of a text fragment may be visible in a wiki, community or identity building are not primary goals of a wiki. So when working in a wiki, most time is spent on content creation, editing, and linking, and not on technology, style, or community-building. As in formal learning settings, the time spent on task is an indicator for good lessons (Meyer, 2003; Helmke, 2005); the reduction of wikis to essential text editing features can be helpful for learning outcomes.

EXAMPLES OF COLLABORATIVE LEARNING SCENARIOS USING WIKIS

Different didactical methods fit different theoretical backgrounds. Active collaborative learning methods fit the theoretical socio-constructive learning background. In CSCL such active collaborative scenarios like Concept-Grid (Dillenbourg and Hong, 2008) or a collaborative glossary (Doebeli and Notari, 2011) are proposed. Such scenarios can be implemented using wikis as a supporting constructive tool. The two proposed collaborative scenarios in this section are just a selection among many. They can be set up using an ABAHCOCOSUCOL model, a progressive inquiry model, or other didactical models and methods.

Collaborative Glossary

Notari (2006) offers a description of an example using the ABAHCOCOSU-COL strategy for a collaborative glossary using a wiki implemented with high school students in a real learning curriculum by one of the authors. Notari notes that after a short description of the unit, the different goals, and the wiki, the participants were asked to search for terms concerning evolution. Then they write a comprehensive definition of the term and publish it on the wiki. A second task was to search through the definitions written by the other students and find similar terms. These terms then were linked to their own definition. A third task was to group similar definitions (example: group all the researchers: Darwin, Lamarck, Cuvier, . . .). After the first contact with the tool, students began to formulate definitions and create new pages. Educators tried to correct mistakes in the definitions, reading texts of the students, giving advice, and helping with the literature and the research on the Web. Educators gave the advice to sign all the inputs and to make references to the literature or the website where they found their information. Students were advised to keep their definitions short and concise.

Students were encouraged to write their own definition. The goal of the dictionary was to create definitions adapted to their state of knowledge. Many definitions they found in the Web were too complicated and full of foreign words. At the beginning they simply pasted definitions found anywhere. After a while they tried more to adapt the definitions they found or at least to explain all the foreign words and difficult sentences. After the first two lessons educators reinforced the linking of concepts. Students had the task of searching for similar words and definitions and trying to link them to other concepts. Educators also told them to complete definitions or to add definitions of terms when this would be necessary while they read the text. They also tried to let the students group similar terms on the start page and build new categories of terms, like, for instance, to group all the researchers. At the end the adults gave them a paper questionnaire and asked them to introduce the answers in a personally created page in the wiki. No special efforts were made to reinforce communication through the tool. Most discussions took place among working pairs orally.

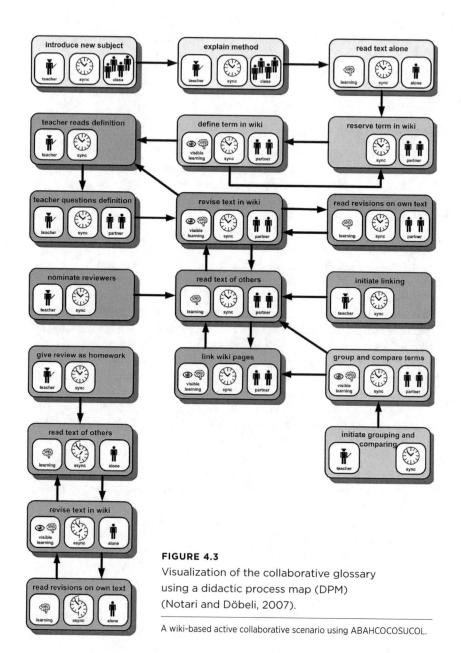

FIGURE 4.3
Visualization of the collaborative glossary
using a didactic process map (DPM)
(Notari and Döbeli, 2007).

A wiki-based active collaborative scenario using ABAHCOCOSUCOL.

CONCLUSION

Collaboration does just not happen per se; an appropriate planning and scaffolding of the curriculum and the singular-learning units is essential for successful learning. The use of wiki functionality supports collaborative elements within a learning unit like the coediting of multimedia artifacts, correcting and commenting on the created texts of others, or being inspired by the work of peers and others. Nonetheless, scaffolding examples comprising collaborative learning units using wikis also need to be adapted to specific requirements of the learning community. Parameters like time frame, age, technology skills, and access to technology and the Internet need specific adaptation for planning and teaching each single course. The example included herein uses a wiki as a tool for collaboration and not a wiki-like tool (e.g., GoogleDocs or Evernote) as described in chapter 1 of this book. One advantage of the use of a wiki is the possibility to create a hypertext structure and to link different pages to each other. Linking similar concepts within the learning topic is an important element following the aforementioned ABAHCOCOSUCOL model. Progressive inquiry and ABAHCOCOSUCOL were conceived for science-related learning topics; with some adaptations, the models can also be used for other domains like language learning, history, geography, culture education, and others.

REFERENCES

Baker, M. J., and K. Lund. 1996. "Flexibly Structuring the Interaction in a CSCL Environment." In *Proceedings of the EuroAIED Conference*, Lisbon, Portugal, 401–7.

Bruner, J. 1960. *The Process of Education*. Cambridge, MA: Harvard University Press.

Chellappa, Ramnath K., and Alok Gupta. 2007. "Managing Computing Resources in Active Intranets." *International Journal of Network Management* 12, no. 2: 117–28.

Cohen, M., and M. Riel. 1989. "The Effect of Distant Audiences on Students' Writing." *American Educational Research Journal* 26, no. 2: 143–59.

Désilets, A., and S. Paquet. 2005. "Wiki as a Tool for Web-Based Collaborative Story Telling in Primary School." *In Edmedia, World Conference of Mulitimedia, Hypermedia & Telecommunication*.

Désilets, A., S. Paquet, and N. Vinson. 2005. "Are Wikis Usable?" In *Proceedings of the International Symposium on Wikis*, 113–16. ACM Digital Library.

Dillenbourg, P. 1999. "What Do You Mean by Collaborative Learning?" In *Collaborative Learning: Cognitive and Computational Approaches*, ed. P. Dillenbourg, 1–19. Oxford: Elsevier.

Dillenbourg, P., and F. Hong. 2008. "The Mechanics of CSCL Macro Scripts." *International Journal of Computer-Supported Collaborative Learning*, no. 3: 5–23. doi: 10.1007/s11412–007–9033–1.

Dillenbourg, P., D. Ott, T. Wehrle, Y. Bourquin, P. Jermann, D. Corti, and P. Salo. 2002. "The Socio-Cognitive Functions of Community Mirrors." In *Proceedings of the 4th International Conference on New Educational Environments,* eds. F. Flückiger, C. Jutz, P. Schulz, and L. Cantoni. Lugano, May 8–11, 2002.

Döbeli Honegger, B. 2005. "Wikis—a Rapidly Growing Phenomenon in the German-Speaking School Community." In *Proceedings of the International Symposium on Wikis.* ACM Digital Library.

———. 2007. "Wiki und die starken Potenziale: Unterrichten mit Wikis als virtuellen Wandtafeln." *Computer und Unterricht* 66. Friedrich Verlag. http://beat.doebe.li/publications/2007-doebeli-honegger-wiki-und-die-starken-potenziale.pdf.

Döbeli Honegger, B., and M. P. Notari. 2011. "Visualizing Learning Processes Using Didactic Process Maps." In *Investigations of E-Learning Patterns: Context Factors, Problems and Solutions,* ed. Christian Kohls and Joachim Wedekind. Hershey, PA: IGI Publishing.

Galbraith, D. 1999. "Writing as a Knowledge-Constituting Process." In *Studies in Writing,* ed. G. Rijlaarsdam and E. Espéret, vol. 4: *Knowing What to Write: Conceptual Processes in Text Production,* ed. D. Galbraith and M. Torrance, 139–59. Amsterdam: Amsterdam University Press.

Guzdial, M., J. Rick, and C. Kehoe. 2001. "Beyond Adoption to Invention." *Journal of the Learning Sciences* 10, no. 3. doi: 10.1207/ S15327809JLS1003_2 .

Hakkarainen, K., and M. Sintonen. 2002. "Interrogative Model of Inquiry and Computer-Supported Collaborative Learning." *Science and Education,* no. 11: 25–43.

Helmke, A. 2005. *Unterrichtsqualität: Erfassen, Bewerten, Verbessern.* Kallmeyer.

Iske, S., and W. Marotzki. 2009. "Reflexivitaet, Proyessualitaet und Partizipation" In *Medienbildung in neuen Kulturraeumen,* ed. M. Bachmair. Springer VS.

Jermann, P., and P. Dillenbourg. 2008. "Group Mirrors to Support Interaction Regulation in Collaborative Problem Solving." *Computers & Education* 51, no. 1: 279–296.

Jermann, P., A. Soller, and M. Muehlenbrock. 2001. "From Mirroring to Guiding: A Review of the State of Art Technology for Supporting Collaborative Learning." In *European Conference on Computer-Supported Collaborative Learning EuroCSCL-2001,* ed. P. Dillenbourg, A. Eurelings, and K. Hakkarainen, 324–31. Maastricht, Netherlands.

Klein, P. D. 1999. "Reopening Inquiry into Cognitive Processes in Writing-to-Learn." *Educational Psychology Review* 11, no. 3: 203–70.

Leuf, B., and W. Cunningham. 2001. *The Wiki Way.* Reading, MA: Addison Wesley.

Meyer, H. 2003. "Zehn Merkmale guten Unterrichts." *Pädagogik,* no. 10: 36–43.

Muukkonen, H., M. Lakkala, and K. Hakkarainen. 2008. "Technology-Enhanced Progressive Inquiry in Higher Education." In *Encyclopedia of Information Science and Technology I–V*, ed. M. Khosrow-Pour, 3714–3720. 2nd edition. Hershey, PA: Idea Group.

Notari, M. P. 2003. "Scripting Strategies in Computer Supported Collaborative Learning Environments." Thesis. University of Geneva. http://tecfa.unige.ch/ perso/staf/notari/thesis_michele_notari_scripting.doc.

———. 2006. "How to Use a Wiki in Education: Wiki Based Effective Constructive Learning." In *Proceedings of Wikisym 2006: International Symposium on Wikis Odense*, 131–32.

Notari, M. P., and B. Döbeli Honegger. 2007. "Didactic Process Map Language: Visualisierung von Unterrichtsszenarien als Planungs-, Reflexions- und Evaluationshilfe." In *Medien in der Wissenschaft*, vol. 44. Waxmann Verlag.

———. 2012. "Wiki: An Archetypical Tool for Collaborative Learning in the Digital Age." In *Wiki Supporting Formal and Informal Learning*, ed. Stefania Bocconi and Giugliemo Trentin (Institute of Educational Technology, Italian National Council, Italy). New York: Nova.

Panke, S., and A. Tillosen. 2008. "Unterwegs auf dem Wiki-Way: Wikis in Lehr- und Lernsettings." www.eteaching.org/didaktik/kommunikation/wikis/08–09–12 _Wiki_Panke-Thillosen.pdf/.

Richardson, Will. 2006. *Blogs, Wikis, Podcasts, and Other Powerful Web Tools for Classrooms*. Thousand Oaks: Corwin.

Schrackmann, I., D. Knuesel, T. Moser, H. Mitzlav, and D. Petko. 2008. "Computer und Internet in der Primaschule." In *Theorie und Praxis von ICT im Unterricht*.

Soller, A. L. 2001. "Supporting Social Interaction in an Intelligent Collaborative Learning System." *International Journal of Artificial Intelligence in Education* 12, no. 1: 40–62.

Suthers, D. 1999. "Representational Support for Collaborative Inquiry." In *Proceedings of the 32nd Hawaii International Conference on the System Sciences (HICSS-32)*, January 5–8, 1999, Maui, Hawaii. CD-ROM. Institute of Electrical and Electronics Engineers (IEEE).

Veerman, A. L., and T. Treasure-Jones. 1999. "Software for Problem Solving through Collaborative Argumentation." In *Foundations of Argumentative Text Processing*, ed. J. Andriessen and P. Coirier, 203–29. Amsterdam: Amsterdam University Press.

Weinberger, A., F. Fischer, and H. Mandl. 2002. "Fostering Individual Transfer and Knowledge Convergence in Text-Based Computer-Mediated Communication." In *Proceedings of the CSCL' 2002*. Boulder, CO, January 7–11.

Wilson, L. R. 2008. "Teaching with Wikis: Towards a Networked Pedagogy." *Computers and Composition* 25: 432–48.

KUNO SCHMID AND
PAOLO TREVISAN

5

Wikis in the Didactics of Science Education

THE SOLOTHURN UNIVERSITY OF EDUCATION IN SWITZERLAND applied wiki uses to the pedagogy of general studies from 2004 to 2008. The inclusion of wikis began with a basic module on world development, "Nature—Man—Contemporaries." This was a two-hour course serving as an introduction to the teaching of general studies. The addressees were 140 students training to be teachers at kindergarten and primary school levels. Around 85 percent of the students were female. The module was prepared and implemented by two lecturers. The lecturers had no previous experience with wikis or other platforms, and just like the students, they were provided with an introductory course and close support from information and communication technology (ICT) professionals. In addition, two classrooms equipped with computers were made available to the students.

PEDAGOGY OF GENERAL STUDIES

The introduction of the course in the pedagogy of general studies was based itself on identifying the requirements of a good general studies class. On the basis of concepts and models that are found in today's general studies lessons, the effective historical approaches of this subject were thematized. The main objective was to enable the students to understand the models of general studies lessons found in current discourse, to relate them to one another, and to discuss these models with regard to their implications for a lesson. Other focal points of the module were the questions of didactic principles and forms of learning, learning objectives and competencies, specific criteria of the learning processes in general studies, and the ways that progress reviews and learning controls are created. The students were taught that keywords alone (e.g., metamorphosis, Romans) are not a good basis for lesson planning. Therefore, they practiced constructing education-related content and topics for teaching, established on the basis of predetermined criteria of educational relevance. They also learned the process of formulating more general questions that require the consideration and connections in knowledge from various related disciplines of general studies

A COURSE WITH WIKI GROUP WORK

The module was designed as a two-hour weekly course for one semester, and the course was divided into two parts with different study formats by the lecturers. The first part was a classical lecture held by the instructors in the form of team teaching. The aim was the teaching of basic and orientative knowledge through a clearly structured course program. The second part was established for collaborative student projects, where the students engaged in learning tasks in groups of five, and a wiki was provided as a tool for the group work. The time spent on the workload for this module was 45 hours, which accounted for 1.5 credit points. In addition to the 14 hours spent in the lectures, 31 hours were designated for reading and group projects. The students spent around two hours on the group work, and they could freely decide when and where to proceed with the project. The lecturers created weekly assignments and advised the students, who formed themselves into around 30 groups (each lecturer was responsible for around 15 groups). They also gave feedback and suggestions on intermediate results and accepted and evaluated the final work. The feedback was delivered partly as written input on the wiki, and partly in the form of personal group discussions. The final performance was measured based on all learning tasks and the thematically structured and designed wiki page of the group. The performance was graded with "met the requirements" or "did not meet the requirements" only.

MOTIVES FOR THE USE OF WIKI

The starting motivation for the use of a wiki was the challenge to accommodate a large number of students in a course, while retaining the quality and commitment of traditional contact studies. The lecturers were looking for a format where meaningful, collaborative self-study could be accompanied by the instructor (*Dossier Selbststudium*, 2006, 7). While the teaching of disciplinary skills, based on the systematics of the subject, should take place during the contact hours, the development and promotion of interdisciplinary skills (such as process designs, individualization of the time required and learning pathways to knowledge acquisition, and cooperative learning) in guided self-study should also play an important role. The students were given time and space to organize themselves and work individually and in groups to finish the given assignments. The lecturers were responsible for guiding the students through educational counseling. To this purpose, a wiki offered good matching possibilities, as it is based on a constructivist teaching-learning-understanding model that enables various combinations of different learning formats in regard to the roles of the students.

The students should experience and apply the didactic principles and constructivist models of the subject presented in the lecture in the sense of "didactic double deckers." Last but not least, the students (mostly young women) had the opportunity to learn and try new forms of digital learning and communication. We had the courage to undertake this venture thanks to the reliable support from the ICT professionals of PH Solothurn (PH Solothurn: University of Teacher Education in Solothurn, Switzerland) and the excellent technical equipment.

VARIOUS USES OF A WIKI

The wiki platform was primarily used as a presentation and discussion medium. The various usage possibilities made the interactive learning task an interesting process. The aim was not about a media-didactic investigation into the new technology, but rather to provide the wiki as an academic didactic tool for study purposes.

Presentation of the Course and Disciplinary Development

Some time before the semester began, the lecturers structured the learning objectives, the content and the planned operation on a wiki page, and forwarded this to the students. Thus, the students were able to get an idea of the course in advance. The content structure was set up with wiki links, so

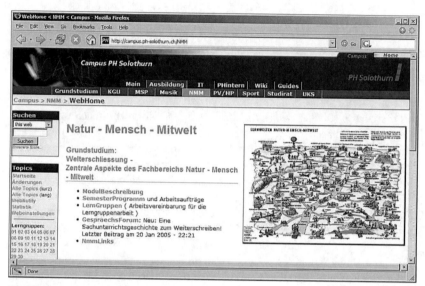

FIGURE 5.1

Home page of the basic module Nature—Man—Contemporaries
(Döbeli Honegger, 2005, figure 2).

that the programs for each lecture and the reading texts could be provided on an attached wiki page. The individual lecture pages served as a valuable storage of documents, as well as providing further reading for the students involved. This also promoted disciplinary developments as the module contents contained diverse educational research and didactic insights. Gradually, an actual wiki discussion developed on disciplinary developments for teaching general studies. The education-related contributions of the various related disciplines of general studies were developed and discussed, creating possibilities for combining different perspectives of general studies. A discussion of "education for sustainable development" (ESD) also resulted in the concept of emphasizing ESD in general studies classes in the following years (Schmid et al., 2013).

The home page represents the starting point of the project. (See figure 5.1.) The main page gives a short introduction and lists the most important links and organizational matters. The bar on the left side provides a search function and lists all contained topics and learning groups, including the corresponding links. The topics are additionally visualized as an environment of "Learning worlds" on the right side of the main page.

Home Pages for Students and Lecturers

Both lecturers took the opportunity to provide links to their own wiki home page on the module home page. They presented information from their

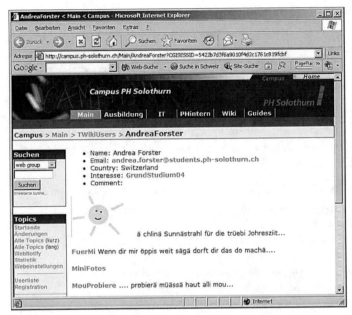

FIGURE 5.2

Personal home page of a female student with links to her
guest book, her photo gallery, and other wiki experiments
(Döbeli Honegger, 2005, figure 4).

curriculum, their roles at the former PH Solothurn, and a list of their pub-
lications. There were no centrally designed employees' websites at the PH
Solothurn, and the lecturers designed their own pages on the wiki-campus,
keeping these up-to-date and deciding for themselves what to present from
their work at the PH Solothurn. At the beginning of the course, the students
were also asked to set up their own wiki home page. Some included only a
mere mention of names, while others tried to put up various information and
pictures during the technical introduction of the wiki. This proved to be con-
tagious. With collegial support the students' pages became more colorful and
complex. They set up guest books and links which connected to one another
and outside sources, while forming their own student network. These communicative possibilities particularly motivated the female students to engage
with the new technology.

Because the students were responsible for the development of their
personal wikis, the content could vary from student to student. Figure 5.2
illustrates the home page of a female student and contains her profile, some
personal statement and images and links to her guestbook, her photo gallery,
and other wikis.

Formation of Work Groups and Cooperative Learning

With regard to the first part of the course, the lecturer set up thirty wiki pages for the work groups that were established as quick links on the home page. Five openings were listed for every work group page. After the first lecture, the students were asked to form into groups of five, open an empty work group page, and fill in the names of the group members. This method of group formation was technically very practical. However, the group dynamics were underestimated in this first implementation. Therefore, in following years, the groups were asked to discuss the form of cooperation and to set up rules. The following aspects had to be defined:

- Where and how shall we conduct the group discussions?
- How shall we ensure that we keep to schedule and meet the deadlines?
- How shall we implement the division of labor, so that all participate equally and with commitment?
- How do we plan to realize the group work by textualization (results, texts, protocols) and in wiki format?
- How shall we deal with conflicts?

The rules agreed by the group had to be formulated in writing and added to the work group page as an attachment. The lecturers and students from other groups were able to view, compare, and make observations. During the course of the lecture, the groups were asked once or twice to reflect on the success of their group work, and the rules were commented upon or adjusted.

The Project of the Work Groups

The main use of a wiki was related to the project of the work groups. Following each weekly lecture, there were reading and learning tasks which had to be completed in the work groups. The groups had to present their results or considerations on their wiki pages through the use of texts and images. In addition, they had to read at least another two groups' pages periodically and write them feedback on the wiki page. The lecturers also followed the wiki presentations and posted critiques, appreciations, or further questions. This made possible collegial support for the learning process, as well as meaningful learning guidance from the lecturers.

Good learning tasks should challenge the students to revise and differentiate their ideas of general studies (Schmid, 2011, 56–57). An example of this is the first assignment from the course. Here, the prior knowledge of each student was activated and made available for processing.

First, answer individually the following questions:

- What is general studies to you?
- Do you remember how this subject was portrayed in your primary school?
- Which content and topics, in your opinion, should belong to general studies? And which should not?
- Think of a typical teaching module that you especially like. Give reasons why.
- Which experiences, knowledge, and skills that you learned at that time were important for your future academic and professional career and your overall personal development?
- What would you have wished to have experienced differently in hindsight?
- Discuss the following questions in your work group and present the answers on the work group page:

  Come up with a single definition for general studies and social studies.

  List all the names for this subject.

  Create a list of topics that are considered "typical" for social studies in school. Highlight the meaningful ones in italics.

  Describe in detail a teaching situation experienced by one of the group members. What was particularly positive or negative in this situation?

The setting of questions was the starting point of the learning tasks. For example, case studies of teaching plans were discussed, texts were selected according to their educational relevance, and questions were formulated in relevance to epochal key topics. The groups worked on their own thematic wiki pages after each lecture. As the wiki pages became more sophisticated, the groups were asked to give a presentation at the end of the semester on a lecture topic based on their work on the wiki pages. The final products were then assessed by the lecturers and each work group received feedback.

Discussion Forums for Emerging Issues in Teaching and Training

Sometimes new questions would come up among the groups as well as in the lectures. These questions were not answered immediately by the lecturers; instead they were presented in the discussion forum. For example, a question was brought to the forum based on a Milka cow illustration: "Agricultural idyll or a beautiful new virtual world: how the cow still remains a topic of General Studies at primary school level in the 21st century." Over the next few weeks, students contributed to this discussion and considered what questions could explicitly deliver knowledge about the cow. However, not every question was discussed with such intensity, and many had only two or three feedback comments, such as the following:

> I find this whole discussion amusing. People in Switzerland support agriculture to a great extent, and the cow plays a very important role for me. Even though the prices for the world market are too high, Switzerland is still breeding cows. This is perhaps "agricultural romanticism," but it is still a huge interest for many. The cow is a logo of Switzerland, and in my opinion, it is closely connected to the history of Switzerland.—Contribution from a student about the Milka cow in the forum.

Following their instruction in teaching methodologies for general studies, the students went on to complete their internship training. The wiki project also allowed the internship trainers to follow the study process of the students and bring forth discussions and practical examples. However, these possibilities were seldom utilized, because the trainers remained critical and reserved toward the wiki project and the new teaching methodologies for general studies.

CONCLUSION

Working with a wiki meant a high degree of independence and cooperation for the students. The part of the lecture that was supported by the wiki tool proved to support and enable constructivist learning. In addition, the wiki project gave many students access to the use of ICT technology. As seen in figure 5.3, the platform was widely used by the students in any case. A major reason for this was the simplicity and openness of the wiki, which allowed the realization of creative and communicative designs.

For the lecturers, two aspects can be seen as significant. First, well-structured and orientated basic knowledge is essential for the success of independent and cooperative learning. Such knowledge can be developed, for example, in a lecture. Secondly, success also depends on relevant and well-defined learning tasks.

The tasks in the work groups were meaningfully and flexibly supported by the lecturers on the platform. However, the necessary time effort should not be underestimated. Overall, the wiki platform functioned as an important contribution to the development of general studies and its didactics.

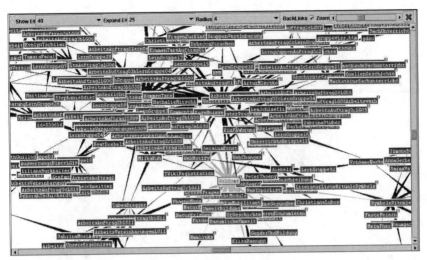

FIGURE 5.3

Excerpt of the wiki networks created during the semester
(Döbeli Honegger, 2005, figure 3).

REFERENCES

Döbeli Honegger, B. 2005. *Wiki und die starken Lehrerinnen.* In *Unterrichtskonzepte für informatische Bildung,* ed. S. Friedrich, 173–83. Lecture Notes in Informatics.

Dossier Selbststudium 2006. www.phzh.ch/dotnetscripts/MAPortrait_Data/ 53733/15/CSPC-Dossier%2004–2008.pdf.

Schmid, K. 2011. *"Religionlernen" in der Schule: Didaktische Überlegungen für einen bekenntnisunabhängigen schulischen Religionsunterricht im Kontext einer Didaktik des Sachunterrichts.* Bern: hep.

Schmid, K., P. Trevisan, D. C. Künzli, and A. Di Giulio. 2013. *Übergeordnete Fragestellung als zentrales Element eines Sachunterricht-Curriculums.* In *SaCHen unterriCHten—Bildung im "Bereich Natur-Mensch-Gesellschaft" in der schweizerischen Lehrerinnen- und Lehrerbildung,* ed. Markus Peschel, Pascal Favre, and Christian Mathis. Hohengehren: Schneider.

MICHELE NOTARI
AND STEFAN SCHÄRER

6

Using Wikis in Project-Based Learning with Groups of More than 100 Learners

THE FOLLOWING CHAPTER DESCRIBES THE USAGE OF A WIKI IN a project-based learning curriculum where over 100 students in groups of three and four worked over two to three months on a project related to the use of media at school. The students were pre-service teachers and undergraduate students at the University of Teacher Education in Bern. The results of this research are also applicable to smaller learning communities in a regular classroom setting.

The curriculum is mandatory for all lower secondary pre-service teachers. The course lasts about eight months. During the first four months, the project is prepared in "traditional lessons." Afterwards the students work in project groups. The total workload for this course is ninety hours; the project work is graded at the end of the course. The importance of practical, "hands on" work for the students is evident. The educational objective of the course is to give an overview and practical competences of teaching and learning with media, to create a set of lessons using media and to practice collaboration in a project-based learning curriculum. The course has been offered for about 100 students annually since 2006. For an overview of the course schedule, see figure 6.1.

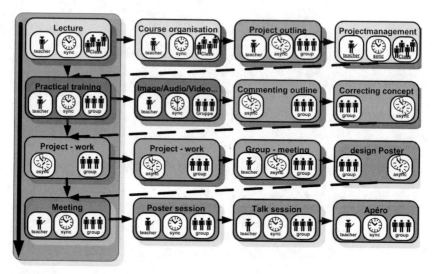

FIGURE 6.1

Didactic process map (Notari and Döbeli Honegger, 2007)
of the media-pedagogy curriculum at the University of Teacher
Education in Bern.

Four phases and selected actions during each phase.

Instructional design was used in order to scaffold collaboration and to embed the use of technology throughout the curriculum. In the first part of the course, lecture (see figure 6.1), the function of technology for the lecture was mainly information transmission (from teacher to students). The focus was to present (e.g., using presentation software) and store lecture information (e.g., by publishing the video of the lecture or the slides). A second important task of technology was to provide learners with information concerning course organization, timeline, and deliverables. For these purposes the course wiki was used. During the lecture phase the students were required to publish an outline of the planned project on the wiki (see figure 6.1). All outlines were visible for all participants. Outlines, concepts and final projects of former students were also accessible on the wiki. The wiki permits editing, commenting, and changing without programming competencies. A short introduction to editing and management of the wiki was provided for those students needing technical support.

In the second part of the course, practical training consisted of "hands on" activities focusing on one medium (audio, image, print, multimedia web, or video). Within this part, practical and procedural competences were acquired. Participants were able to apply and reflect on the focus of course media in different school-related situations.

TABLE 6.1

Descriptions of the icons of figure 6.1.

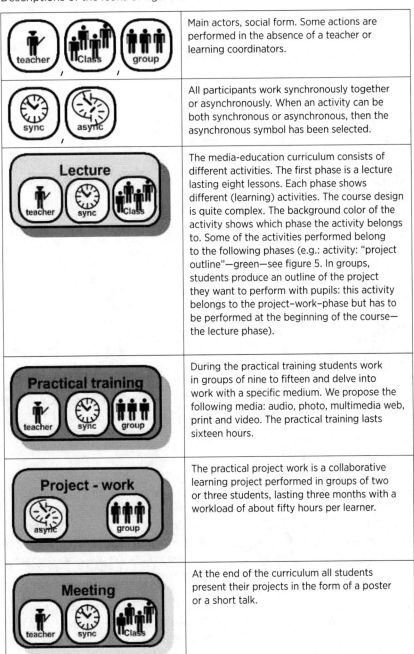

teacher, Class, group	Main actors, social form. Some actions are performed in the absence of a teacher or learning coordinators.
sync, async	All participants work synchronously together or asynchronously. When an activity can be both synchronous or asynchronous, then the asynchronous symbol has been selected.
Lecture — teacher, sync, Class	The media-education curriculum consists of different activities. The first phase is a lecture lasting eight lessons. Each phase shows different (learning) activities. The course design is quite complex. The background color of the activity shows which phase the activity belongs to. Some of the activities performed belong to the following phases (e.g.: activity: "project outline"—green—see figure 5. In groups, students produce an outline of the project they want to perform with pupils: this activity belongs to the project–work–phase but has to be performed at the beginning of the course—the lecture phase).
Practical training — teacher, sync, group	During the practical training students work in groups of nine to fifteen and delve into work with a specific medium. We propose the following media: audio, photo, multimedia web, print and video. The practical training lasts sixteen hours.
Project - work — async, group	The practical project work is a collaborative learning project performed in groups of two or three students, lasting three months with a workload of about fifty hours per learner.
Meeting — teacher, sync, Class	At the end of the curriculum all students present their projects in the form of a poster or a short talk.

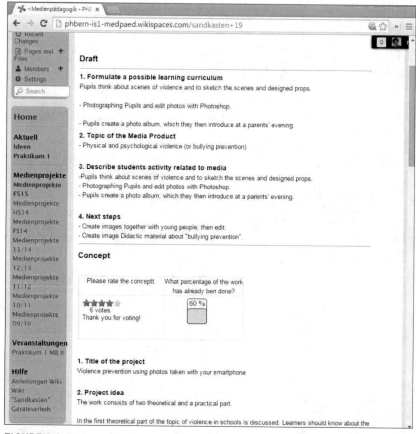

FIGURE 6.2

Concept website with the required elements.

The role of technology within this phase differed depending on the type of selected training (audio, video). Participants in the multimedia training checked different current communication and web-publication tools and concepts. Participants in the audio and video training got to know several concepts for treating audio and video and related tools. The photo group used digital image processing software, and the print group were introduced to different text-processing tools and concepts. The syllabus of all training courses was published on the wiki. Students' exercises were also published and visible for all participants. No mandatory cross-course peer interaction mediated by the wiki environment was scheduled. Within some training courses, peer interaction in the form of formative feedback, comments, and collaborative content creation were planned and supervised by the teacher. Students who were involved in the same project group during the third phase of the curriculum attended the same practical training course. They had to discuss the earlier published outline of their project with the teacher. The outcomes of the discussion were also published on the wiki. Once the outline had been approved by the teacher, the project groups started to formulate a concrete concept of their project. A list of requirements was provided for the publication of the concepts on the website, like "project title," "project idea," "goals," "target group," "theoretical background," "time schedule," "infrastructure needed at school," "what will the pupils learn during the prepared courses," "pupils activities during the lessons," and "amount of lessons." Each group had an own editable concept website where the required concept elements are visible (see figure 6.2).

The group members edited the concept directly in the template. The site was editable by all participants of the course. Each saved version could be recovered. All participants could rate the concept using a five-star rating widget.

Third Part: Project Work

The third part of the course consisted of the production of a concrete sequence of a certain amount of school lessons based on their experience from the practical training course. The first deliverable of the project work was to publish a concept of the project on the wiki. After that a peer review cycle was launched. Each participant had to comment on two concepts of other groups. The comments were published on the discussion page of the commented concept (see figure 6.3).

Knowledge building was supported by creating the collaborative artifacts and then reading other project sites and concepts, commenting on them and integrating the good ideas of other concepts in the personal project. The instructional model of the whole curriculum is called "action based hypertext-constructing computer supported, collaborative learning model" (ABAH-COCOSUCOL, Notari, 2006).

The project groups worked independently during the following three months. There was one mandatory work package (intermediate milestone) to be performed before the final project was published on the wiki. The groups had the opportunity to ask for a group meeting with the teacher and every published project step was visible on the website. Some students published the ongoing project collaboratively using the wiki page as a common work space. Some students visited the wiki pages of other groups in order to find inspiration for their own work.

A template was proposed for the publication of the final project. Similar to the concept, different key elements were mandatory, like "Title," "Abstract," "characteristics of the projects," "tags," "amount of lessons," "infrastructures," "pupils activities," . . . (see figure 6.4). Some groups used the project page to

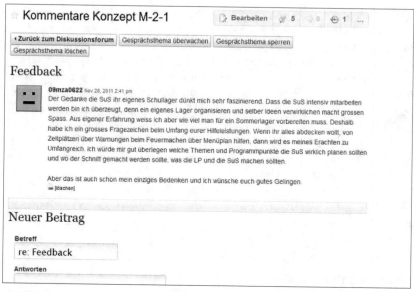

FIGURE 6.3

Example of the discussion page of a concept site.

The concept was reviewed by six people. The teacher also formulated a review for the group members.

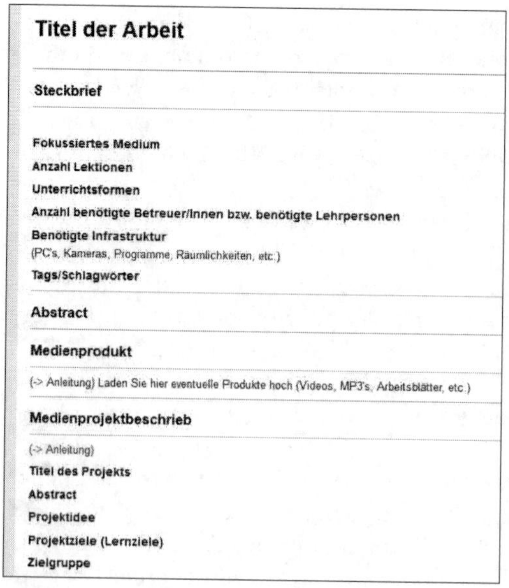

FIGURE 6.4

Template of the project-description page.

Learners have the possibility to use the template in order to be sure that they do not forget important elements of the project description. Every year, 35–45 projects are added to the wiki page. Using a similar structure for all the projects makes it easier for students and teachers to search for specific projects.

write their contributions collaboratively. Most groups used common local word-processing tools and exchanged the files using e-mail. The importance of chat and SMS (Short Messages sent over mobile phone, using the GSM Network) to coordinate project management has increased over recent years. Further longitudinal studies are planned in order to detect the development of communication and collaboration habits of learners in such a project-based learning setting. The end of the project work is an individual reflection around the product, the collaboration within the group, and the satisfaction with the project.

The fourth part of the course consisted of the presentation of the works in a meeting. ICT is used to produce the posters and to sustain the talks, and we planned to set up a "meeting weblog" or a "meeting wiki" for the communication among the participants.

All posters and all products remained online and accessible for everybody on the Web.

EXPERIENCES

The wiki has been used for over three consecutive curricula with a total amount of students of over 300. Over 6,000 pages have been created and edited and over 1,200 files have been uploaded. A total amount of 137 group projects have been performed, including an approximate workload of 200 hours per project. All projects were visible and available to all students.

QUANTITATIVE ANALYSIS OF THE USAGE OF THE WIKI

The wiki management functionality of the wiki spaces allows one to visualize the usage behavior of the single learners and the learning groups. Among other options it is possible to see how groups divided tasks of the project, and who edited which part of the work. These functionalities (metadata) allow the teacher to scaffold students' activities during the ongoing learning process and may also help for the final assessment. The teacher may also discuss the performed actions within the wiki with the learners or with the project groups.

The following two examples show which data can be retrieved using the offered wiki history site metric:

Page views: Total amount of page views of each page of the Wiki.

Edits: Amount of edits and changes performed each side of the Wiki.

The edits and page views are counted for each day and can be exported for further processing.

Page Views during the Project Work

Figure 6.5 shows the page views during the time where students were performing their projects (cohort 2010/11). In order to understand the following figures, it is important to mention that the 100 students were divided into four groups for the practical training. The practical training groups 1 and 2 started before and were followed by the practical training groups 3 and 4. Therefore there were different deadlines of delivery of the specific milestones and final project for groups 1–2 and 3–4 (see table 6–2).

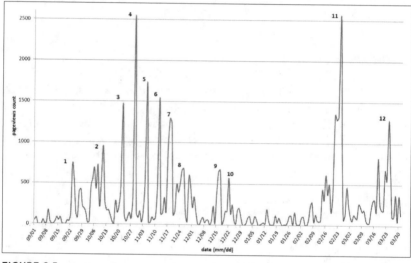

FIGURE 6.5
Page views cohort 2010/11.

The activity monitoring within the wiki shows that (as expected) the students were very active when they were delivering artifacts. The activity during the practical trainings was also high. Students learned to interact with the tool in this project phase.

The difference in the page view activity of point 11 and 12 is due to the fact that groups 1 and 2 consisted of more participants than groups 3 and 4.

The page views per student are comparable for the groups 1 and 2 and groups 3 and 4 (see table 6.3).

TABLE 6.2
Page views cohort 2010/11.

No.	Specific event within the curriculum	Page views 2010/11
1	Individual log-in to the wiki sent to students	736
2	Deadline for milestone 1: publication of a scratch of the project	953
3	First practical training (see phase 2: practical work)	1,470
4	Second practical training	2,584
5	Third practical training	1,729
6	Fourth practical training	1,544
7	Publication of a concept for the project (groups 1 and 2)	1,296
8	Peer feedback (groups 1 and 2)	685
9	Publication of a concept for the project (groups 3 and 4)	672
10	Publication of a concept for the project (groups 3 and 4)	245
11	Deadline for project delivery (groups 1 and 2)	2,562
12	Deadline for project delivery (groups 3 and 4)	1,283

TABLE 6.3
Page views per student in the different trainings (cohort 2010/11).

	Page views per student	Page views per project group
Training 1 and 2	23.48	67.62
Training 3 and 4	19.33	51.56

The comparison of the two cohorts 2009/10 and 2010/11 shows slightly different activity patterns in the last week before the deadline for project delivery (see figure 6.6).

Figure 6.6 shows the activity of students a few days before the deadline for concept delivery. Students of the cohort 2009/10 delivered the concept closer to the deadline than students of the cohort 2010/11. Students of the cohort 2010/11 received an e-mail one week before the deadline. They were more active within this week on the wiki. Being more active shows that they may have seen concepts of other groups and had the opportunity to improve their work.

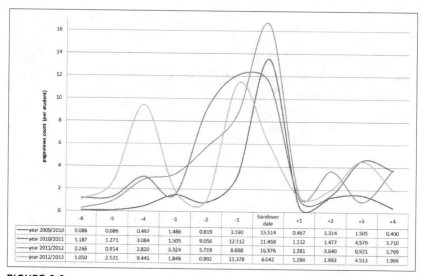

	-6	-5	-4	-3	-2	-1	handover date	+1	+2	+3	+4
year 2009/2010	0.086	0.086	0.467	1.486	0.819	3.190	13.514	0.467	1.314	1.505	0.400
year 2010/2011	1.187	1.271	3.084	1.505	9.056	12.112	11.458	1.112	1.477	4.579	3.710
year 2011/2012	0.266	0.914	2.820	3.324	5.719	8.698	16.576	1.381	3.640	0.921	3.799
year 2012/2013	1.050	2.521	9.445	1.849	0.992	11.378	6.042	1.286	1.992	4.513	1.966

FIGURE 6.6

Comparison of the last week before delivery deadline of the concept works (cohort 2009/10 to 2012/13).

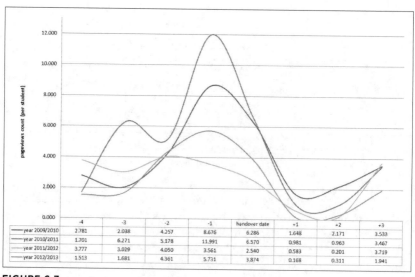

	-4	-3	-2	-1	handover date	+1	+2	+3
year 2009/2010	2.781	2.038	4.257	8.676	6.286	1.648	2.171	3.533
year 2010/2011	1.701	6.271	5.178	11.991	6.570	0.981	0.963	3.467
year 2011/2012	3.777	3.029	4.050	3.561	2.540	0.583	0.201	3.719
year 2012/2013	1.513	1.681	4.361	5.731	3.874	0.168	0.311	1.941

FIGURE 6.7

Delivery of the project work of practical training groups 3 and 4 of the cohorts 2009/10 to 2012/13.

Figure 6.7 shows students' activity in proximity to the deadline for project work delivery. Most students seemed to publish the work around the deadline, with maximum activity on the day of the deadline. We made a minimal scaffolding adaptation in the cohort 2010/11. Students had to deliver their work as Wiki—Text. We interceded to upload just a word file as final project work. We expected this intervention to lead to greater activity in the week before the deadline.

Students Editing Behavior

Besides page views, the editing behavior within the wiki is a good indicator for students' activity during work. We note that the two parameters are interrelated; a student cannot edit a page without visiting and viewing it.

Figure 6.8 and table 6.4 show the editing behavior of students during the whole project phase.

Students of the cohort 2010/11 edited the wiki pages earlier than students of the cohort 2009/10. We expected that the earlier increasing activity was due to the fact that the cohort 2010/11 had to deliver the project as wiki text and was not allowed just to upload a word file (see figure 6.9).

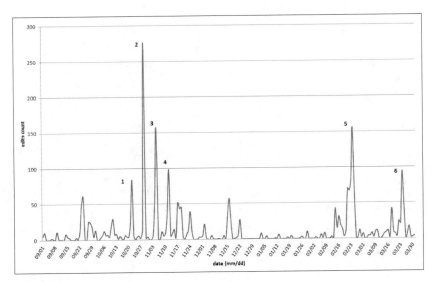

FIGURE 6.8
Amount of page edits for the cohort 2010/11.

TABLE 6.4

Amount of page edits for the cohort 2010/11.

No.	Scaffolding event	Page edits
1	First practical training (groups 1 and2)	84
2	Second practical training (groups 1 and 2)	276
3	Third practical training (groups 1 and 2)	157
4	Fourth practical training (groups 1 and 2)	98
5	Deadline for the project (groups 1 and 2)	156
6	Deadline for the project (groups 3 and 4)	

As expected, the editing activity of students is comparable to student page views during the curriculum. The amount of page views is more elevated than the amount of edits.

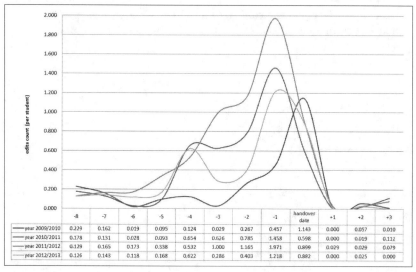

	-8	-7	-6	-5	-4	-3	-2	-1	handover date	+1	+2	+3
year 2009/2010	0.229	0.162	0.019	0.095	0.124	0.029	0.267	0.457	1.143	0.000	0.057	0.010
year 2010/2011	0.178	0.131	0.028	0.093	0.654	0.626	0.785	1.458	0.598	0.000	0.019	0.112
year 2011/2012	0.129	0.165	0.173	0.338	0.532	1.000	1.165	1.971	0.899	0.029	0.029	0.079
year 2012/2013	0.126	0.143	0.118	0.168	0.622	0.286	0.403	1.218	0.882	0.000	0.025	0.000

FIGURE 6.9

Comparison of the amount of edits around the deadline for project delivery for the cohorts 2009/10 to 2012/13.

Editing Behavior within the Project Groups

The total amount of page views and edits do not indicate how the working activity was divided within a project group. Wikispaces Wiki offer a functionality to detect the number of edits for each participant. For our setting each participant had a personal log-in, so we could detect how the edit repartition among the different project groups was. We also wanted to find out if all group members showed the same activity (homogeneous edit repartition within a project group). We used the coefficient of variation (CoV) within a project group to describe the wiki edit homogeneity within the group.

CoV = group standard deviation/group mean × 100

A CoV value > 100 means a big editing heterogeneity among project groups. In figure 6.10 shows a comparison of the CoV of the cohort 2009/10 and the cohort 2010/11.

Astonishingly, the cohort 2010/11 had a higher heterogeneity in the editing behavior within the project groups (see figure 6.10). The more heterogeneous the editing behavior within a group is, the more the tasks have been split within a group. The more homogeneous the editing behavior, the more the group interacts using the wiki and has the opportunity to co-write and compare the ongoing work.

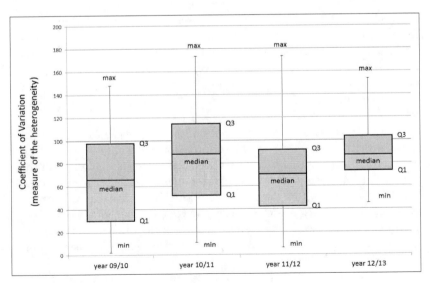

FIGURE 6.10

Box-plots editing heterogeneity of the project groups.

CONCLUSIONS

In addition to the displayed activity charts, we asked students about their working/collaboration behavior during their project activity. The groups stated they used three to four weeks for the project work (instead of the supposed three-month project activity). We recommend to introduce more milestones in such project activities where students have to publish some elements of the project. The more such elements are visible on a common wiki, the more the learners have the opportunity to see what other participants of the learning community have performed and the more they can learn for their own work.

In addition to use of the wiki, the groups interacted for their project work with the following tools: Dropbox (https://www.dropbox.com), Boxnet (http://box.net), Educanet (http://educanet.ch) and BSCW (http://bscw.de).

Project-based learning (PBL) normally takes place in classroom-sized learning communities of 20 to 30 students. From teachers' perspective, compared to traditional learning units, PBL is rather work-intensive teaching. Besides the setting up of the project environment, learners need a lot of scaffolding work during the project and intense monitoring. In our setting with over 100 learners, the tutoring and commenting, scaffolding, and managing activities were proportionally higher than in a classroom setting; we also needed to keep track of the projects' deliverables, comment upon student work, and give personal feedback for the different work phases.

We tried to organize the work around the wiki as a publishing, commenting, and managing environment for the projects. Over the duration of the research, we noticed that the delivery management was not optimal if we just published deadlines and delivery examples on a specific wiki page. It turned out to be much more efficient if we sent e-mails to all participants around one week before the deadline for a specific milestone. Within the e-mail we just placed a link to the wiki page where the roadmap and the delivery of the milestones were published.

Setting more and smaller milestones where students had to publish parts of the project also turned out to be fruitful for the quality of the delivered projects. We were aware of the fact that more milestones led to more commenting and managing work. So we started to introduce peer review tasks as specific milestones within the project work. We hoped to make students more aware of different projects of the learning community and saved a notable amount of time we were supposed to spend writing comments on each project. Students had the opportunity anytime to ask for specific feedback on a produced project artifact.

The wiki as a publishing environment turned out to be very efficient for the monitoring of the progress of the projects, for the commenting and peer feedback milestones, and for students' learning how to manage a specific task within the project. How much control and how much freedom is fruitful for the quality of a project depends on the age and motivation of the learners. Younger novices and less motivated students needed more scaffolding and control than highly motivated students, who are experienced in project-based learning units.

Learning Process Analytics

Introducing the wiki as technology enhancement for the project-based learning unit enhanced the opportunity for collaborative writing and efficient project monitoring and management. Using the user activity features of Wikispaces also empowers teachers to see what the learners do at which time of the project phase and enables teachers to react appropriately and individually while the project is ongoing.

From the point of view of the learner, it turned out to be helpful to have tools permitting a quick overview of the ongoing work of other members of the learning community. We created a visualization elements (so-called webwidgets) where project groups could see at a glance to what extent a milestone of the project was fulfilled (work in progress widget; see figures 6.12 and 6.13). We also introduced a widget where students could rate the ongoing project page using a five-star rating (rating widget; see figure 6.11) and a visualization element, where all the work rating and "work in progress" widgets were taken together (meta-widgets; see figure 6.14) (Notari et al., 2013).

FIGURE 6.11
Rating widget, introduced on each project page for each important milestone of the project work.

FIGURE 6.12
"Work in progress" widget (dropdown for the input).

The project group members had to declare the percentage of the fulfilled task. The widget was displayed on each project page for each important milestone of the project work.

FIGURE 6.13
"Work in progress" widget (read-only view for all members of the learning community).

13HS - Bild						
Bereich	Konzept	Konzept	Konzept	Projekt	Projekt	Projekt
Gruppe	Bewertung	Fortschritt	Link	Bewertung	Fortschritt	Link
B-1-1_13	★★★★★ 3 votes	100 %	Konzept ►	★★★★★ 0 votes	100 %	Projekt ►
B-1-2_13	★★★★★ 4 votes	100 %	Konzept ►	★★★★★ 0 votes	100 %	Projekt ►
B-1-3_13	★★★★☆ 3 votes	100 %	Konzept ►	★★★★★ 0 votes	60 %	Projekt ►
B-2-1_13	★★★★★ 0 votes	100 %	Konzept ►	★★★★★ 0 votes	100 %	Projekt ►
B-2-2_13	★★★★☆ 3 votes	100 %	Konzept ►	★★★★★ 0 votes	100 %	Projekt ►
B-3-1_13	★★★★★ 5 votes	100 %	Konzept ►	★★★★★ 0 votes	0 %	Projekt ►
B-3-2_13	★★★★☆ 5 votes	100 %	Konzept ►	★★★★★ 0 votes	20 %	Projekt ►
B-4-1_13	★★★★☆ 3 votes	100 %	Konzept ►	★★★★★ 0 votes	40 %	Projekt ►

FIGURE 6.14
Meta widget (Bewertung = rating, Fortschritt = project state) of all projects.

The meta widget has been displayed on the entry page of the wiki. Students could navigate directly to the specific project page using the (Konzept/Projekt) link.

REFERENCES

Notari, M. P. 2006. "How to Use a Wiki in Education: Wiki-Based Effective Constructive Learning." In *Proceedings of Wikisym 2006: International Symposium on Wikis Odense*: 131–32.

Notari, M., and B. Döbeli Honegger. 2007. "Didactic Process Map Language: Visualisierung von Unterrichtsszenarien als Planungs-, Reflexions- und Evaluationshilfe." In *Gesellschaft für Medien in der Wissenschaft*. Medien in der Wissenschaft, vol. 44. Münster: Waxmann.

Notari, M., S. Schär, M. Schellenberg, and S. Chu. 2013. "Empowering Formative Assessment Using Embedded Web Widgets in Wikis." In *Proceedings of the 2013 Joint International Symposium on Wikis and Open Collaboration (WikiSym + OpenSym 2013)*. ACM.

MANOLI PIFARRÉ

7

How to Use a Wiki in Primary Education to Support Collaborative Learning Processes

SOCIAL TECHNOLOGIES HAVE BECOME KEY FEATURES OF LEISURE and work places, and also are starting to have a key role in education. Web 2.0 technologies have opened up new possibilities for open learning (Cole, 2009). In a short time we have shifted from a static Web in which users had a passive role to a dynamic, collaborative, and participatory Web in which users have an active role, creating and sharing knowledge in a global web setting.

Different authors have agreed that Web 2.0 classes need to emphasize a learning culture based on participation, collaboration, creativity, dialogue, and knowledge creation (e.g., Wegerif, 2007; Pifarré and Kleine Staarman, 2011). We claim in this chapter that a dialogic perspective is in need in order to use Web 2.0 technologies to support collaborative knowledge-construction processes in primary education. From this point of view, one main issue in primary education is how to support our students to create and be engaged in powerful, critical, and reflective dialogues using Web 2.0 technologies that help them to co-construct new knowledge through online interaction with others.

Therefore, the objective of this chapter is to show how primary teachers can use the potential of a wiki environment for supporting students' development of an intersubjective orientation toward one another and to support the creation of a "dialogic space" to co-construct new understanding. To this end, we will show how we designed, implemented, and evaluated a science project in which twenty-five primary students used a wiki environment, with the specific aim of establishing and supporting collaborative interaction, while engaging in a collaborative science writing task.

LEARNING TO LEARN TOGETHER IN A WIKI: HOW TO DEVELOP STUDENTS' COMPETENCIES RELATED WITH PARTICIPATION, INTERACTION, DISCUSSION, AND COLLABORATION

Collaborating and being involved in a collaborative knowledge activity in a wiki is necessary to develop, through social interaction, a "dialogic space" in which students can think and act collectively and can open up a space between people in which creative thought and reflection can occur. In order to help students to create the necessary "dialogic space" in a wiki, teachers need to develop educative wiki projects that provide resources, opportunities, and scaffolds for children to work and talk together, and for expanding, deepening and widening online interaction with others. From our perspective, in order to develop productive online interactions in a wiki that could enhance collaborative learning, wiki projects in primary education should include activities that explicitly support students in the following three aspects:

- The promotion of "exploratory talk" (Mercer, 2000)
- The establishment of ground rules for productive and reasoned dialogues
- The development of argumentation in online dialogues

The Promotion of "Exploratory Talk"

Mercer (2000) argues the importance of language as a basic thinking tool which allows negotiating and group thinking. The development of language functions as a tool of thought is deeply related to its social use. As Mercer claims, "language is designed to carry out processes far more interesting than simply conveying information. It allows the involvement of individual mental resources with a collective and communicative intelligence which lets the users perceive the world in a clearer way and develop practical ways to deal with it."

Through a detailed study of the interaction between students during small group work, Mercer identifies three types of talk:

> *Disputational talk,* which is characterized by disagreement and individualized decision making. There are few attempts to pool resources, or

to offer constructive criticism of suggestions. Disputational talk also has some characteristic discourse features—short exchanges consisting of assertions and challenges or counter-assertions.

Cumulative talk, in which speakers build positively but uncritically on what the other has said. Partners use talk to construct a "common knowledge" by accumulation. Cumulative discourse is characterized by repetitions, confirmations, and elaborations.

Exploratory talk, in which partners engage critically but constructively with each other's ideas. Statements and suggestions are offered for joint consideration. These may be challenged and counter-challenged, but challenges are justified and alternative hypotheses are offered. Compared with the other two types, in exploratory talk knowledge is made more publicly accountable and reasoning is more visible in the talk.

The development, implementation, and evaluation of the program called "Thinking Together," which proposes activities to help students to be aware of the features of exploratory talk and its benefits for group work, has experimentally shown that the presence of exploratory talk characteristics in a small group situation is correlated with a better resolution of the group task and more success in the process of individual reasoning. Besides, the characteristics of exploratory talk are related to the promotion of collaborative learning processes (Mercer and Littleton, 2007; Dawes, Mercer, and Wegerif, 2000).

In this chapter, we claim that the "thinking together" approach can also help students to develop online collaborative processes and to support the co-construction of new understandings in a wiki environment.

The Establishment of Ground Rules for Productive and Reasoned Dialogues

Class interaction is determined by a set of conversation rules established by the members (teacher and pupils). However, these rules often remain implicit, and many students find it hard to communicate in an effective way during the development of the classroom tasks and to use language as a reflective and learning tool. Some studies state that it is necessary to help these pupils and give them the chance to be aware of the interaction and communication rules they use.

Mercer and colleagues have identified a set of conversation rules which they call "ground rules" that are created by the group and promote an exploratory type of talk (Mercer and Littleton, 2007; Dawes, Mercer, and Wegerif, 2000). The "ground rules" that allow organizing a small group discussion which favors the presence of exploratory talk features are the following seven ones:

1. All relevant information is shared.
2. The group seeks to reach agreement.
3. The group takes responsibility for decisions.
4. Reasons are expected.
5. Challenges are accepted.
6. Alternatives are discussed before a decision is taken.
7. All in the group are encouraged to speak by other group members.

Even though all these programs with rules that can promote an exploratory talk have been developed during face-to-face classroom lessons, the inter-thinking and collaborative knowledge constructions that they promote can also be applied to written communication contexts (Wegerif and Dawes, 2004) where a written communication with exploratory characteristics can enhance a positive experience in collective thinking and knowledge building. This is what we want to achieve in our work and in using a wiki.

Therefore, we have adapted a set of activities based on the program "Thinking Together" as a strategy to promote exploratory talk in the wiki environment as a way to help students to collaboratively construct new knowledge.

The Development of Argumentation in Online Dialogues

Apart from considering the rules of conversation for oral and written interaction and promoting peer interaction oriented to exploratory talk, we think that teachers should take into account another type of scaffolding to reinforce the practice of collaborative interaction based on inter-thinking and intersubjectivity that can promote dialogue in a wiki environment with a high educational value.

The use of "sentence openers" (see table 7.1) can help students with an argumentative conversation (Ravenscroft and Matheson, 2002). These sentences are intended to guide the discussions that the pupils have to deeper, more critical and grounded stages. In providing specific "sentence openers" to the students, we intend to help promote an interaction and negotiation between students based on the argumentation of ideas, critical thinking, and a rich knowledge construction.

In the next section, in the description of our educative project, it is explained how these "sentence openers" have been worked out with the pupils in order to promote a better discussion and negotiation of ideas in the wiki environment.

To conclude this section, from our point of view, to stimulate learning through collaborative writing tools as a wiki, it is necessary first to give support and promote the processes and skills involved in the dialogue, the negotiation and exchange of ideas in a constructive way.

TABLE 7.1

Examples of "sentence openers."

Inform	Question	Challenge	Reason	Agree
I think . . .	Why is it?	I disagree because . . .	Are you saying that . . . ?	I agree because . . .
Let me explain:	What do you mean when you say . . . ?	I'm not sure . . .	Therefore . . .	That's right!
Because . . .	What do you think about . . . ?	Another view might be . . .	I think both are right because . . .	Do we all agree?
An example:	Can you give an example?	I think something different . . .	To summarize . . .	We have all agreed that . . .

THE DESIGN OF AN EDUCATIVE PROJECT THAT USES A WIKI IN PRIMARY EDUCATION TO SUPPORT COLLABORATIVE LEARNING

Wikis are a particularly helpful lens through which to reexamine the role of argumentation, collaboration, critical interaction, and new media writing. But the enhancement of higher learning processes with wikis is not granted by only using them, because the design of a specific educative environment is required.

In order to prepare our primary students to argue and write collaboratively about science topics in a wiki environment, we designed an educative process with the following three educational phases:

Phase 1. *Thinking together and developing face-to-face collaborative skills.* The main objective of this phase was to promote exploratory talk.

Phase 2. *Learning about the topic students will write in the wiki.* Using *inquiry web-based methodology* as a pedagogical tool to learn about the content that students will argue and write on in the wiki.

Phase 3. *Arguing and writing collaboratively in a wiki environment.* Wiki environment design. In this phase students share the knowledge learned during the second phase and build together a collaborative text about a topic.

In figure 7.1, we summarize the three phases of the educative project, and in the next section we will explain in detail each phase of our educative program.

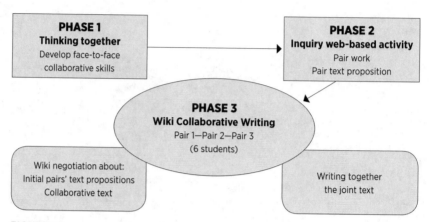

FIGURE 7.1
Phases of the wiki educative project.

Thinking Together and Developing Face-to-Face Collaborative Skills

To promote collaboration among pupils, it was initially considered a work based in oral interaction by the use of recreational dialogical situations. This becomes the key point of the work proposal because it is considered the essential learning that students must achieve so they can later transfer it to the wiki.

The oral interaction proposal had the aim to promote discussion and collaboration among pupils so that they could later transfer the acquired skills when working with the wiki. The given situations come from the "Thinking Together" (Dawes, Mercer, and Wegerif, 2000) program, which covers a range of activities designed to achieve an exploratory talk.

In our project, we chose a series of everyday situations. Students had to discuss them in small groups and face-to-face. We encourage them to reason and argue in their discussions and to develop productive dialogue in order to reach a group agreement to solve the everyday situation. Next we present an example of these situations to promote dialogue and exploratory talk features.

Situation

> In the playground, during the break time, two kids, Albert and Cristian, have broken the window glass of a class while they were playing football. Enric has seen how everything happened. Albert and Cristian have asked Enric not to say anything to the teacher.

Teachers guarding the playground have come to ask what has happened and who did it.

Rosa, one of the teachers who has witnessed the accident

And knows Enric was near there, asks him

If he knows something . . .

Enric doesn't know what to do. On the one hand, Albert and Cristian are his friends and he doesn't want to get them in trouble, but on the other hand he doesn't want to lie and get in trouble with teacher Rosa.

What would you do? Would you tell the teacher?

In order to improve and enrich the discussion, a set of "sentence openers" (consult table 7.1) were presented to the pupils so that they could experience how to use them in order to improve their discussion.

The purpose of using these expressions is that pupils can learn how to talk in a richer way, structuring their thoughts and sharing them with the rest of the pupils.

To help students use and incorporate these "sentence openers" in students' discussions, we proceeded as follows:

First, the teacher explained to the whole class the different kinds of expressions listed in table 7.1, distinguished by colors depending on five aims: giving information, asking questions, comparing, contrasting opinions, and reasoning. Together, the teacher and the pupils negotiated and agreed on the purpose of each of the expressions and then gave an example of how and when they could use them. These examples, listed in table 7.1, were put in five cards with different colors pertaining to the different dialogue objectives, and the cards were placed in the middle of the small group work space. Each group also had the information about the utility of these expressions.

After that, the teacher showed in the whiteboard the situation to discuss. She did a general reading of the situation to make sure that everybody understood it. Before proceeding with the conversation in small groups, the aim that had to be achieved when holding the conversation was remembered: reaching an agreement that gave a solution to the problem. The children were encouraged to use as many expressions as they could to enrich the discussion.

During the development of the task, the teacher guided pupils' work, going through all the groups and helping them to develop their talk and leading it to a higher level; in other words, promoting an exploratory talk.

Once all the groups had provided a "solution" to the situation, each group exposed to the whole class the agreements reached during the discussion, their arguments, and summarized the development of the task (what was their general impression, how had the cards helped, which expressions they had used the most, etc.).

PHASE 2

Learning about the Topic Students Will Write in the Wiki: Inquiry Web-Based Methodology as a Pedagogical Tool to Learn about the Content That Students Will Argue and Write Collaboratively in the Wiki

Prior to meeting in the wiki environment and writing about a scientific topic, students learned about the content and the topic they should argue about and write in the wiki. From our point of view, the way that students learn the facts of the field that they have to discuss is another key educational point. In order to build good argumentations students must construct, coordinate, and evaluate scientific knowledge. To reach this objective, we used an inquiry web-based methodology in which students learned about the content in a meaningful and constructive way. From our point of view, the fact that students learned the topic in a constructive and meaningful way can help them in sharing, discussing, and arguing about their knowledge.

To this purpose, students followed and solved a WebQuest activity. In this activity students searched the Internet and learned about a science topic. Each WebQuest activity asks students specific questions related to a science topic. At the end of this stage, every pair of students wrote an initial proposition giving some ideas related to the science question stated in the WebQuest activitiy. This text pops up as initial proposals from which to start the negotiation and composition processes in the wiki.

Readers can find examples of the inquiry web-based activities designed in our project on the Web: www.contic.udl.cat/en; and in Pifarré (2010).

PHASE 3

Using a Wiki to Collaboratively Write a Science Text

In this section, we will describe the wiki environment designed, as well as the educative use of the wiki.

The Wiki Environment Designed

In our project, we used the Wiki-Media engine. The wiki space includes two frames divided into a vertical position. The bar that separates them is movable, so students can adapt the space according to their needs.

The left frame is consultation space and contains two tabs: (a) instructions to use the wiki and (b) the students' initial ideas. These initial ideas were those texts written in the second phase of our project and as a solution of the

WebQuest activity which pop up as initial proposals from which to start the negotiation and composition processes in the wiki. The right frame is writing space and it includes the negotiation page and group page: these two sections are those that, apart from being read, can be edited and consulted from the history. Let us examine each one of these sections in more detail.

Consultation Space: Instructions

In our wiki space, instructions are displayed at the beginning of the use of the wiki and students can consult them whenever they need it.

There are two main sections in the instructions tab. The first one consists of a conceptual map which explains the main objective of the wiki—that is, to write a group text using the negotiation page and the group page. The second section explains the procedure of how to better work in the wiki environment. Three main steps are explained: 1st Read, 2nd Negotiate, 3rd Write together in the group page. Finally, some pieces of advice on editing are presented and the function of the history page is explained (figure 7.2).

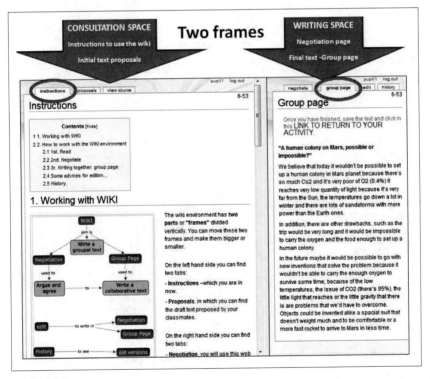

FIGURE 7.2
Wiki environment: instructions and group page.

Writing Space

In this section, students can negotiate and reach a consensus on how to write the final text. An example of a negotiation process is shown in figure 7.3.

The instructions suggest that students explain the arguments of their contributions in the negotiation space, so their partners can better understand their ideas. Also, some pieces of advice are provided to negotiate by means of openers, in order to remember the preparatory activity about developing face-to-face collaborative argumentation skills.

Also, in the writing space students can write the text collaboratively in the group page (figure 7.3). This joint process leans on the negotiation process carried out before and during the writing of the text. Students are encouraged to explain to their wikigroup partners what changes have been made in the collaborative text and why, in order to facilitate the work of the group and to favor social awareness and group self-regulation, a critical feature in collaborative writing.

In order to write a text together in the wiki, we followed the following educative process:

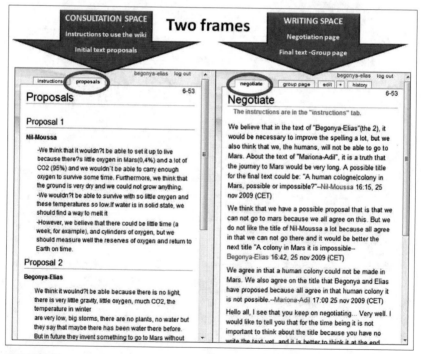

FIGURE 7.3

Wiki environment: proposals and negotiation spaces.

(a) Every three pairs join in the same wiki space to write the argumentative text collaboratively. These three pairs of students form a wikigroup.

(b) The three-pair initial proposals of the text that the students wrote in the WebQuest activity appear automatically in the wiki environment, in the consultation space.

(c) Students could write simultaneously in the negotiation frame and/or in the group page. The teacher encouraged students to negotiate and reach an agreement about their ideas in the negotiation frame.

(d) The group page is reserved for the group final text. In order to show quickly to the others the changes made in the group page, students must report the changes introduced in the group page in the negotiation frame.

(e) The teacher also made contributions to the wiki negotiation page at the beginning or at the end of each session. The objectives of the teacher's contributions were

- To summarize students' contributions
- To focus the work of the session in order to move forward in the collaborative activity
- To guide the use of the wiki negotiation process and the wiki collaborative writing framework

How Students Worked in the Wiki

Students worked in the wiki during six class sessions. Students always work in pairs. Every three pairs joined in the same wiki space or wikigroup. Pairs of the same group took turns to work in the wiki for periods of about 10–15 minutes. This way of working avoided editing conflicts in the wiki.

At the beginning, the teacher strongly encouraged students to use the "sentence openers" as an aid to help them to start a contribution in the wiki negotiation space. A set of "sentence openers" were also in the wiki, in the instructions section of the wiki (see table 7.1).

Especially at the beginning, students needed the help of the teacher, who was constantly guiding the technical aspects and the writing process. The teacher became involved in the process—co-learner—by contributing ideas and trying to help during the writing process. Nevertheless, her contributions started decreasing as the students gained expertise in using the wiki environment.

Students were encouraged to focus on the following aspects:

1. The construction of common ideas for the final text rather than on surface aspects of the writing. Because students were not used to reading texts from their partners, at first they focused their attention on spelling mistakes, but progressively students began focusing on meaning and how to organize the collaborative text (Pifarré and Fisher, 2001).

2. To justify the ideas and/or opinions provided.
3. Check if the contribution has been signed.

When performing the first sequence of work with the wiki, the need to create some participation rules arose. Accordingly, the different groups established their own rules for participation in the wiki. Examples of these rules are: "We need to work together to go as fast as possible," "We have to justify our points of view and agreements," "There has to be an agreement between the couple and with the rest of the group," "Before making any decision, things have to be discussed with the other couples," "There must be a respect for other couples' opinion," and so on.

DESCRIPTION OF THE COLLABORATION PROCESS FOLLOWED BY THE STUDENTS IN THE WIKI ENVIRONMENT

Basically, the collaborative process that the pupils followed when working with the wiki can be summarized in four episodes or stages:

EPISODE 1

Generation of Ideas

In this first episode, the aim for the students seemed to be to generate shared content and to plan the collaborative writing process. Students only wrote in the negotiation space and the contributions of students indicate an exploratory orientation. The three pairs in each group had to write a joint text, and in doing so, they had to make sure they discussed all the ideas that were present in each of the initial text proposals that each pair wrote in phase 2 of our educative project. These text proposals were products of the solution of the inquiry web-based activity that students undertook in order to learn about the content of the text that they had to write collaboratively in the wiki.

This stage became a key stage for drafting the final text because it is where they reach agreements with regard to the collaborative writing of the text. It has the following processes:

- Reading of the other couples' initial proposals.
- Brainstorming of common ideas about the initial texts to look for agreements regarding the writing of the final text.
- Discussion of arguments in order to claim an idea in the common text (Is it possible to establish a human colony on Mars or isn't it?, for example). It also includes the discussion and justification

of ideas, the generation of doubts about confusing information, and so on.

- Contribution and organization of the ideas that should be reflected in the final text.

EPISODE 2
Text Generation: Additional Ideas

This episode focused on the joint generation of text and as such, the students' contributions are mainly featured in the group space, in which the joint informative text was written. In this part of the task, the three pairs that composed each wiki group took turns in writing the collaborative text. The three pairs contributed actively to the writing of the collaborative text. The students in this episode were mainly involved in adding those ideas that were agreed upon in the previous episode. In all the wiki groups, one pair seemed to take the lead at the start of the writing process and took a coordinating role. The other two pairs were more focused on improving the text by adding new arguments to the collaborative text, and expanding or reorganizing previous ideas.

EPISODE 3
Text Drafting: Expansion and Enrichment of the Text

In the third episode, the students were engaged with the sharing of new ideas to deepen and widen their existing texts. Students wrote both in the negotiation page and in the group page and their contributions were written with the following three collaborative purposes:

1. To share new ideas for the collaborative text, which were presented with reasons and arguments.
2. To discuss the arguments written in the text. Although students did not delete ideas from the collaborative text, they did contribute critically, identified inconsistencies in others arguments, and proposed alternatives. In addition, they expressed their disagreements in the negotiation space, and waited for the pair who had written the idea to change, correct, or remove it. Even so, in general, students were very respectful of each other's ideas.
3. To make visible their thinking and explain to the others what they had written in the collaborative text. Students gave explicit reasons for the changes they had made in the collaborative text. In doing so, the students made their knowledge more publicly accountable and their reasoning became more visible in the negotiations.

EPISODE 4

Finishing the Collaborative Text

This last episode was focused on coordinating key activities and ideas in order to finish the joint text. In the last stage, students focused on aspects like choosing the title, clarifying some ideas that might still not be clear, and so on.

EVALUATION OF THE QUALITY OF THE WIKI COLLABORATIVE TEXTS

We analyzed some features of the collaborative text written by the students using the wiki environment. To do so, we compared the first text proposition written by the pairs in the second phase of the project and the collaborative text written by students using the wiki environment in the third phase of the project. Our intention was to examine some quantitative features that could indicate in what ways the collaborative process analyzed in the previous sections had influenced the ways in which the initial pairs' ideas were incorporated, deepened, and widened in the final group text. Specifically, we compared the length (i.e., number of words) of the different texts, the number of t-units; the number of scientific ideas and the number of reasoning connectors (e.g., because, however, if, but, also, besides, for example, moreover). In our work, a t-unit is the shortest grammatically allowable sentence into which writing can be split. Often, but not always, a t-unit is a sentence.

In terms of number of words and t-units, it must be highlighted that students' contributions are longer in the collaborative text group than in each of the initial texts written by the pairs. Moreover, the longer texts are richer and more accurate, based on an increase in the number of t-units.

Moreover, the structure and organization of the ideas in the collaborative text also seem more accurate than in the initial texts. Students organized their ideas in different paragraphs and they introduced a title and a conclusion.

The number of reasoning connectors also increased in the collaborative text compared with the pairs' initial text propositions. We argue that this is another indicator that demonstrates that the students went deeper into argument chains, elaborated upon the meaning of arguments, and better understood the concepts involved.

From our perspective, this analysis indicates that the product of students' collaborative work is more than the sum of the initial pairs' work. We claim that the collaborative processes developed by students in the wiki environment, which, as we demonstrated earlier, was characterized by openness of ideas and the widening and deepening of a creative dialogic space, may have been an important factor in helping the students to write a joint, collaborative text.

CONCLUSIONS

Our project highlights the unique ability of a wiki to support collaborative argumentation. This chapter shows evidence that wikis can create a dialogical space where students share knowledge, reasons, and arguments about a science topic. This common space helped students who participated in our project to work constructively together and collectively write an argumentative text with high levels of scientific accuracy.

We reported that students worked collaboratively in the wiki negotiation space and showed an exploratory orientation to others in which partners engage critically yet constructively with each other's ideas. Statements and suggestions were offered for joint consideration. Knowledge was made more publicly accountable, reasoning was visible in the collaborative space, and explicit reasons about one's own ideas were provided.

In this chapter we argued the necessity to design an instructional approach that prepares students to use wiki capabilities as a powerful tool capable to mediate collaborative science argumentation. A pedagogical use of the wiki's capabilities is needed in order to foster negotiation and argumentation abilities in primary students. From our point of view, it is crucial to develop students' awareness about thinking and working together. To reach this objective, our study showed that the "thinking together" approach (Mercer, 2000) was effective in this preparation. Students transferred onto the wiki negotiation space some features of exploratory talk and thinking-together skills.

Moreover, our work also showed the effectiveness of scaffolding argumentation through dialogue games. In our study students used effective prompts to structure their interaction in the wiki and to promote a dialogue based on reasoning and argumentation.

ACKNOWLEDGMENTS

This project was funded by the Ministerio de Ciencia y tecnología of the Spanish government (project numbers: SEJ2006–12110; EDU2009–11656). The author would like to thank the teacher and their students for their participation in the work reported in this chapter.

REFERENCES

Cole, M. 2009. "Using Wiki Technology to Support Student Engagement: Lessons from Trenches." *Computers & Education* 52: 141–46.

Dawes, L., N. Mercer, and R. Wegerif. 2000. *Thinking Together: A Programme of Activities for Developing Thinking Skills at KS2*. Birmingham: Questions Publishing.

Mercer, N. 2000. *Words and Minds: How We Use Language to Think Together.* New York: Routledge.

Mercer, N., and K. Littleton. 2007. *Dialogue and the Development of Children's Thinking: A Sociocultural Approach.* London: Routledge.

Pifarré, M. 2010. "Inquiry Web-Based Learning to Enhance Knowledge Construction in Science: A Study in Secondary Education." In *Computer-Assisted Teaching: New Developments,* ed. B. A. Morris and G. M. Ferguson. New York: Nova.

Pifarré, M., and R. Fischer. 2001. "Breaking Up the Writing Process: How a Wiki Can Support the Composition and Revision Strategies of Young Writers." *Language and Education* 25, no. 5: 451–66.

Pifarré, M., and J. Kleine Staarman. 2011. "Wiki-Supported Collaborative Learning in Primary Education: How a Dialogic Space Is Created for Thinking Together." *International Journal of Computer-Supported Collaborative Learning* 6: 187–205.

Ravenscroft, A., and M. P. Mathenson. 2002. "Developing and Evaluating Dialogue Games for Collaborative e-Learning Interaction." *Journal of Computer-Assisted Learning.* Special issue: "Context, Collaboration, Computers and Learning" 18: 93–102.

Wegerif, R. 2007. *Dialogic Education and Technology.* New York: Springer.

Wegerif, R., and L. Dawes. 2004. *Thinking and Learning with ICT: Raising Achievement in Primary Classrooms.* London: Routledge.

SAMUEL KAI WAH CHU,
NICOLE JUDITH TAVARES,
CELINA WING YI LEE, AND
DAVID WILCK KA WAI LEUNG

8
Using a Wiki for Collaborative Learning at Primary Schools

WITH RAPID TECHNOLOGICAL ADVANCEMENT AND WITH THE fact that the new generation is born in the digital era, integrating Web 2.0 technologies (e.g., blogs, wikis) into education has been seen as beneficial in facilitating learning and teaching (Chu, Chan, and Tiwari, 2012; Chu and Kennedy, 2011; Richardson, 2006). A wiki, "a collaborative web space where anyone can add content and anyone can edit content that has already been published" (Richardson, 2006, 8), is a popular Web 2.0 technology used in the field of education. Studies on the application of wikis at different levels and domains of education have revealed their benefits to students at large (e.g., Chu, 2008; Fung et al., 2011; Law et al., 2011; Li et al., 2010; Mak and Coniam, 2008; Pifarré and Starrman, 2011; Tavares and Chu, 2011; Woo et al., 2011). Pifarré and Starrman (2011) point out that wikis open up shared dia-logic space for students to discuss one another's ideas, thus scaffolding their critical thinking and problem-solving skills. In addition, through the exchange of ideas or peer comments on wikis, not only have students been proven to be able to give constructive feedback on the content and language use of their own work (Mak and Coniam, 2008; Woo, Chu, and Li, 2010), resulting in collaboration and enhancement of work quality (Chu, 2008), but also to have developed social skills in the course of the negotiation of meaning (Fung et al., 2011).

Teachers have also been found to benefit from this technology. With the revision history function in wikis, teachers can monitor the contribution and engagement of students in a group's work which provides sound evidence for them to assess students' performance objectively, and offer support and immediate guidance whenever necessary (Chu, 2008; Woo et al., 2011; Yu et al., 2011). Nevertheless, for effective wiki-supported learning to take place, a carefully formulated pedagogical approach to students' and teachers' knowledge of wikis' functionality, group size, and strategies for motivating peer-learning are needed (Engstrom and Jewett, 2005). This chapter thus aims to provide an instructional design for the implementation of wikis in the primary school classroom, with illustrations from two studies conducted by the authors, one on general studies group project work (Law et al., 2011; Yu et al., 2011) and the other on English collaborative writing (Fung et al., 2011; Tavares and Chu, 2011), both of which utilize a wiki as the platform. Recommendations are also given to primary teachers should they wish to consider integrating wikis into their own classrooms.

WIKIS IN UPPER PRIMARY CLASSROOMS

With support from the Quality Education Fund backed up by the Education Bureau in Hong Kong (http://qefpblp.pbworks.com/w/page/31127656/FrontPage), the research team was able to apply the use of a wiki to support general studies group project work and English collaborative writing at the Primary 5 level (grade 5 in other educational systems) in four primary schools in Hong Kong.

In our deliberation over a wiki for Primary 5 students in Hong Kong, we arrived at the decision that a wiki with a multilingual interface covering both Chinese and English would be desirable. Since the language and cognitive abilities of primary students are in the developing phase, we expected that a wiki bearing the mother tongue (Chinese) of primary students would allow them to have better control over the technological applications, since English is a second language in Hong Kong. Among the popular wiki platforms (e.g., Mediawiki, Pbworks, and Google Sites), only Google Sites provides an interface supporting various languages, including Chinese and English. Therefore, Google Sites was selected to be the wiki platform in the two studies, appealing to the Primary 5 students who can utilize the Chinese interface for their general studies group project where classes are conducted in Cantonese while they can enjoy the flexibility of choosing either the Chinese or English interface for their English collaborative writing project.

To ensure effective collaboration among students using Google Sites in the classroom, a careful teaching plan was then devised. This section describes the pedagogical approach adopted to facilitate the implementation of Google Sites in primary schools, on the basis of the two studies conducted on the Google Sites-supported general studies group project work and Google Sites-supported English collaborative writing at Primary 5 level in four schools in Hong Kong.

General Studies Group Project Work

Instructional Design

Primary 5 students from four primary schools in Hong Kong participated in the study in which they were required to work on a general studies group project using Google Sites, lasting for a period of 2–3 months. The four schools, including FK, HS, SP and KS, decided on a different topic and their students were encouraged to work collaboratively using the Google Sites web page only accessible to the corresponding school.

A collaborative teaching approach was adopted in the study in which the general studies teacher, teacher librarian, Chinese language teacher, and information technology (IT) teacher worked with concerted effort to equip their students with the skills necessary for completing their project on the wiki platform. The first term was spread out over a period of twelve weeks, within which the teaching and learning activities were introduced and carried out. At the end of the twelve-week period, the students would have completed their general studies projects and be ready for presentations, preferably using their wiki site. All the teaching and learning activities in the timetable were expected to contribute toward the students' final project output.

The general studies teacher oversaw the entire project learning and trained students with research skills and basic knowledge relevant to their project. The general studies teachers were encouraged to collaborate with IT teachers and exchange information about students' learning progress and their project titles. Essentially, the general studies teacher helped the IT teacher determine the relevant information and communication technology (ICT) skills students would need when carrying out their general studies group projects on the wiki platform.

IT teachers were in charge of teaching students basic knowledge about using Microsoft PowerPoint, such as inserting pictures and video clips, using spreadsheets, and the creation of charts. To support the inquiry projects, students were introduced to the basic skills in using a wiki platform. This teacher with technological expertise taught students various functions of Google Sites based on the *Handbook of Google Sites* (Chu, Law, et al., 2010) published by the research team before the start of the general studies group project to familiarize students with the new technology and platform.

As information is abundant on the Internet, to narrow down the search results to specific information, the teacher librarian played a key role in teaching students how to locate information through utilizing keyword search skills and keys such as "OR" and "AND." Apart from familiarizing students with various searching strategies, the teacher librarian was also responsible for teaching students how to use WiseNews to search for news and magazine articles.

Once students identified the right piece of information, they were guided in expressing it in their own words. As copying and pasting information from the Internet was strongly discouraged during the entire project, the Chinese teacher was delegated the task of developing students' paraphrasing and summarizing skills through comprehension tasks to facilitate their understanding of topic sentences and central ideas in each paragraph. Chinese teachers could employ reading materials that were related to the research areas of students' general studies projects.

Students' and Teachers' Perceptions

A survey on four areas, namely, learning/pedagogy, motivation, group interaction, and technology, along with in-depth interviews were conducted to collect students' opinions. In general, students were observed to hold positive attitudes toward the effectiveness of Google Sites in their learning.

Learning/Pedagogy

In the survey, statements such as "I will retain more material as a result of using the Wiki" and "Use of the Wiki aided me in achieving course objectives" were included. A majority of the students gave the statements high ratings, revealing that they believe Wiki technology fosters learning among them.

Motivation

Because they were able to employ different media to present the general studies group project on Google Sites, for example, by using pictures and video clips, students were perceived to be more motivated to complete the given tasks. This in turn raised their interest in the subject matter that they were researching, as shown by the survey that most students believed that "I stayed on task more because of using the Wiki." This finding is further endorsed by the observation of teachers from KS who noted that weaker students, who were originally unable to complete their work using the traditional approach, became more enthusiastic about their work and succeeded in producing work of higher quality when Google Sites was used in their project.

Group Interaction

Students acknowledged that it was more convenient to communicate with their group members on Google Sites, as one student commented: "Before using Google Sites, we had to speak to one another before deciding what to edit, which was very inconvenient. With Google Sites, we now just have to post our concerns on the Web and everyone can see it." This shows that Google Sites provides a platform that facilitates group interaction.

Technology

Students enjoyed using Google Sites to do their projects. With Internet access, students reported working on their projects "anytime and anywhere." They can also search for and edit information easily, as a student who compared using Google Sites to the traditional approach remarks, "Google Sites is better because we can easily locate all the information we need online." Unlike using a word processor (e.g., Microsoft Word) where students have to work their own space and time, on Google Sites they can work on the project with their group members simultaneously and exchange views through the site, which adds to the overall convenience. As suggested by a student from KS, "If I were the teacher, I would definitely introduce Google Sites to students because it is very convenient. If we use Word to do our projects, we have to do it separately, but we can all do the work at the same time on Google Sites."

ENGLISH COLLABORATIVE WRITING

Instructional Design

Similar to the above study, Primary 5 students from the four primary schools took part in the research study on English collaborative writing. Students were first required to co-construct a piece of writing in English on paper in the first term to develop their collaboration skills, and then on Google Sites in the second term to experience the new technology. The four schools, including FK, HS, SP, and KS, differ from one another in terms of the number of classes involved, the composition topic students wrote on, and their implementation plan.

In the first term, during week 1, students acquainted themselves with the pen-and-paper collaborative writing task by learning how to evaluate their own writing, searching for relevant sources and brainstorming ideas, drawing mind-maps in groups, peer-evaluating the content of their writing, focusing on the level of interest it generates and the relevance of their ideas to the given topic. As soon as students received feedback from their peers and the teacher, they began writing in groups in week 2 and revising their mind-maps. Afterwards, there was a second peer evaluation cycle with an emphasis on the organization of ideas in their writing. Along with their teacher's feedback, the students continued refining their co-constructed work. In week 3, a third peer-evaluation task was introduced in which language use was the central focus. With this feedback from both their peers and the teacher, students made revisions to grammar and vocabulary and finalized their writing. A final evaluation was then administered by the teacher to find out students' individual level of enjoyment and contributions to the task. This enabled the teacher to bring this collaborative experience to a close with more room for reflection.

Since students were required to engage themselves in collaborative writing using Google Sites in the second term, apart from learning what was mentioned in week 1 of the first term, they learned how to use the Google Sites writing platform. In week 2, based on the feedback given by their peers and the teacher on Google Sites, students began writing in groups on the site and revising their mind-maps based on given feedback. The subsequent steps for weeks 2 and 3 resembled that of the pen-and-paper writing task in the first term.

Because peer and teacher evaluations contribute significantly toward the quality of the students' final work, professional development workshops were organized for teachers taking part in the study to empower them with the confidence to conduct process writing in their classrooms and to provide timely as well as constructive feedback on their students' writing in both the pen-and-paper format and via Google Sites. At the workshops, the teachers' knowledge of the writing process, approaches to the teaching of writing, their role in facilitating learning, and the giving of quality feedback were strengthened. In particular, the teachers were reminded of the importance of having a clear set of assessment criteria and ways of guiding their students in interpreting the criteria and evaluating one another's written work with the help of different evaluation templates. The workshop organized during the intervention provided the opportunity for the teachers from the four schools to come together again to share and reflect on their experience of their tryouts in phase 1, to compare the evaluation templates they used and their impact on the quality of students' written work, to voice their concerns, and to collectively plan ahead for phase 2. What was notable about this workshop was that teachers received feedback on the comments they made on their students' work, discussed the impact of their use of prompts, questions, suggestions, and revisions in different forms, and explored how they could maximize the benefits of their strategy use. In addition to the training provided to teachers, students were also taught how to evaluate a piece of writing, depending on their prior experience and knowledge. Teachers were encouraged to familiarize their students with the evaluation criteria to sharpen their critical thinking skills in evaluating their peers' work too.

Students' Perceptions

Group interviews were conducted to gather students' opinions. In general, students shared a positive attitude toward the use of Google Sites in facilitating collaborative writing. Peer learning was both welcomed and valued in the collaborative process while the use of technology (features of Google Sites) was favored by students.

Peer Learning

Among the many advantages of using Google Sites, students stressed the avenue it created for them to leave comments on one another's work, thereby promoting peer learning and enhancing their interpersonal skills. While completing the collaborative writing project, through giving their peers feedback on aspects such as spelling, grammar, flow of ideas, and the logic of their presentation, students were presented with ample opportunities to evaluate others' work and reflect on their own, leading to improved quality of their writing. This echoes the findings in the study conducted by Chu (2008). Figure 8.1 (see page 104) shows the comments made on language use by various students in a class and the corresponding revisions made on the writing (marked by colored words).

In addition, there is clear evidence of mutual appreciation among students and weaker students learning from their more capable counterparts, as one student noted: "If we use Google Sites as the collaborative platform, we get to read the pieces of writing from other classes, exchange views and comment on our classmates' work. If we write on paper, we can only read a few pieces." So students in general welcomed having the chance to share their work on Google Sites.

What was even more encouraging to find was clear evidence of students learning from and with one another through the process. As illustrated by the following example, a student wrote "Your writing is good but I do not [understand] the meaning of truthful" after reading his classmate's work and the writer responded by saying, "truthful means honest."

Technology

In line with the study on the Google Sites-supported general studies group project, students enjoyed using Google Sites to compose their English writing, as expressed by two participants of the study: "When we use Google Sites, all our group members can do the project at the same time, unlike using Microsoft Word. This makes things simpler and easier to manage." On the whole, students have not reported major difficulties using Google Sites, and have found it convenient to work with their group members and edit their writing there.

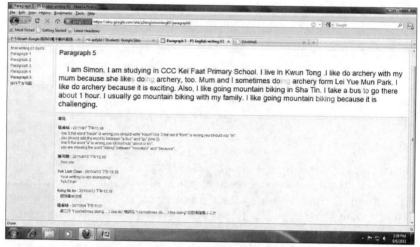

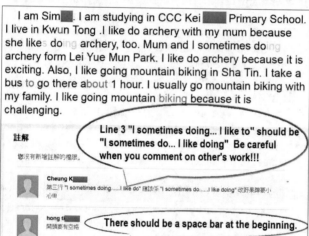

FIGURE 8.1

Comments made on grammar by various students and the corresponding revisions made by the group on their writing (marked by words in different colors).

RECOMMENDATIONS
FOR PRIMARY SCHOOL EDUCATORS

With regard to the benefits of using wiki on primary students, teachers may consider experimenting with wikis in their teaching. Acknowledging the fact that wikis are relatively new to teachers and technical challenges and parental concern over using wikis were found in our current and previous research studies (Chu, 2008; Fung et al., 2011; Law et al., 2011; Woo et al., 2011; Yu et al., 2011), a few practical recommendations on these areas are put forward to primary teachers to facilitate their trial.

Choosing a Wiki

There are many existing wiki platforms but they vary in terms of the interface, level of access, price, and so on. A wiki platform which is easy to use, requires minimal computer knowledge, and has a multilingual interface may be preferable. Primary students can therefore choose the language they are most comfortable with and this can ease their cognitive load, thereby allowing them to focus on the content of their work. In addition, a wiki platform free of charge is essential for educational purposes.

Providing Technological Support

A range of studies have shown students encountering technical problems in areas such as the formatting of the content of their writing and uploading materials onto wikis (Chu, 2008; Fung et al., 2011; Law et al., 2011; Woo et al., 2011). For effective learning to emerge, teachers may need to decide if extra or supplementary classes need to be organized for students to reduce their fear of using wikis before starting them off on a project.

Addressing Parental Concerns

When students are using wikis for their projects, they may be misunderstood by their parents as visiting websites or playing online games (Fung et al., 2011; Law et al., 2011; Yu et al., 2011). It may therefore be advisable for schools to run workshops for parents to introduce them to this new mode of learning so as to ease their potential worries. These workshops can enable parents to deepen their knowledge of the operation of wikis and learn ways to monitor their children's work, as suggested in Law et al. (2011). Before the implementation of wikis in the classroom, schools may also find it helpful to inform parents of wiki-related tasks their children will be performing at home.

CONCLUSION

Learning in a wiki environment is becoming more widespread. Studies on the Google Sites-supported general studies group project and Google Sites-supported English collaborative writing in Hong Kong have demonstrated that primary students found Google Sites easy to use and enjoyed the benefits Google Sites created in terms of their overall learning, motivation, and peer learning. In order for effective collaborative learning with wiki to work in the everyday classroom, this chapter describes the instructional design of adopting wikis in education, with illustrations from the two aforesaid studies, and provides recommendations for primary school teachers to consider when using wikis.

REFERENCES

Chu, S. 2008. "TWiki for Knowledge Building and Management." *Online Information Review* 32, no. 6: 745–58.

Chu, S. K. W., C. K. K. Chan, and A. F. Y Tiwari. 2012. "Using Blogs to Support Learning During Internship." *Computers & Education* 58, no. 3: 989–1000.

Chu, S., and D. M. Kennedy. 2011. "Using Online Collaborative Tools for Groups to Co-Construct Knowledge. *Online Information Review* 35, no. 4: 581–97.

Chu, S. K. W., A. H. C. Law, M. K. T. Choi, M. Y. K. Mak, and B. L. F. Pun. 2010. *Handbook of Google Sites.* Hong Kong: Centre for Information Technology in Education, Faculty of Education, University of Hong Kong.

Chu, S. K. W., N. Tavares, F. L. C. Siu, K. Chow, S. Y. Ho, and M. K. T. Choi. 2010. *Teaching Guide for Teachers on Inquiry Based Learning: Primary 5 General Studies Project Learning and English Collaborative Writing.* Hong Kong: Centre for Information Technology in Education, Faculty of Education, University of Hong Kong.

Engstrom, M. E., and D. Jewett. 2005. "Collaborative Learning the Wiki Way." *TechTrends* 49, no. 6: 12.

Fung, K. Y., S. K. W. Chu, N. Tavares, G. Ho, and K. Kwan. 2011. "Using Google Sites in English Collaborative Writing. Paper presented at CITE Research Symposium 2011, University of Hong Kong, Hong Kong.

Law, H. C., S. K. W. Chu, F. Siu, B. Pun, and H. Lei. 2011. "Challenges of Using Google Sites in Education and How Students Perceive Using It." Paper presented at CITE Research Symposium 2011, University of Hong Kong, Hong Kong.

Li, X., S. K. W. Chu, W. W. Ki, and M. Woo. 2010. "Students' and Teacher's Attitudes and Perceptions toward Collaborative Writing with Wiki in a Primary Four Chinese Classroom." Paper presented at the 3rd International Conference "ICT for Language Learning," Florence, Italy.

Mak, B., and D. Coniam. 2008. "Using Wikis to Enhance and Develop Writing Skills among Secondary School Students in Hong Kong." *System* 36: 437–55.

Pifarré, M., and J. Kleine Starrman. 2011. "Wiki-Supported Collaborative Learning in Primary Education: How a Dialogic Space Is Created for Thinking Together." *Computer-Supported Collaborative Learning* 6: 187–205.

Richardson, W. 2006. *Blogs, Wikis, Podcasts and Other Powerful Web Tools for Classrooms*. Thousand Park, CA: Corwin.

Tavares, N., and S. Chu. 2011. "Experimenting with English Collaborative Writing on Google Sites." *Proceedings of the QEF Project Dissemination Symposia.* "Applying a Collaborative Teaching Approach to Inquiry Project-Based Learning with Web 2.0 at Upper Primary Levels." Hong Kong, June 30.

Woo, M., S. Chu, A. Ho, and X. X. Li. 2011. "Using a Wiki to Scaffold Primary School Students' Collaborative Writing." *Journal of Educational Technology & Society* 14, no. 1: 43–54.

Woo, M., S. Chu, and X. X. Li. 2010. "Tracing Peer Feedback to Revision Process in a Wiki-Supported Collaborative Writing." In *The Second Asian Conference on Education*, 1881–98.

Yu, C. T., C. S. Fong, W. K. Kwok, S. M. Law, S. K. W. Chu, and I. Ip. 2011. "Using Google Sites in Collaborative Inquiry Projects in General Studies. Paper presented at CITE Research Symposium 2011, University of Hong Kong, Hong Kong.

REBECCA REYNOLDS

9

Wikis as Learning Management Systems for Computer Science Education in Intermediate and Secondary Schools

THIS CHAPTER DISCUSSES WAYS IN WHICH A WIKI-BASED learning management system can be employed to support middle school and high school students' digital project-based work, including game design and creation, file management, collaboration and information-seeking, toward their development of introductory computer science expertise and digital literacy. In the program discussed, middle school- and high school-aged students learn how to design interactive web games about a school subject or about a subject of personal interest, by taking a game design class daily, for credit and a grade for an entire school year. They work individually and in teams to successfully design a game, while using a wiki-based learning management system (LMS) to support their knowledge building, in a blended learning modality. In this guided discovery-based learning program, students rely upon each other, the LMS resources, and their teacher for instructional guidance.

The LMS learning resource was built upon MediaWiki architecture, and has been advanced and developed iteratively over several years by a nonprofit organization to its present state today, as a game design curriculum called Globaloria. The wiki-based LMS includes features such as tutorials for learning game design and introductory programming, a set of sequenced learning units, assignments and curricula, social media tools, file archiving features, learning logs, a progress timeline, and a rewards system that assigns points and titles to students as they complete each task and activity.

To investigate student wiki uses, a research study was conducted, drawing upon Google Analytics data that reports the frequency of student page reads to varying URLs on the LMS. Findings help the researchers as well as participating teachers and program staff better understand ways in which students and schools vary in their utilization of the range of resources to support their game design learning and development. Data generated by Google Analytics as well as the automatically generated reports in MediaWiki offer behavioral trace evidence of student wiki uses that support progress tracking, assessment, and evaluation. The aim of this evidence-based practice is to arm teachers and instructional designers with metrics that can enable diagnostics on student learning processes, and lead to improvements in teacher and system design scaffolding toward more successful learning outcomes.

This chapter provides an overview of the theory underscoring the game design program's deployment of this wiki-based LMS, and addresses ways in which the wiki-based LMS has been implemented. The chapter also highlights study findings on student wiki uses, and offers a discussion of the use of site metrics for assessment of student engagement and resource uses. The "Discussion" section summarizes the opportunities presented to educators in using wikis to support students' collaborative knowledge building, computational thinking, and digital literacy.

BACKGROUND

The learning theories influencing the design of the game design program we describe below include social constructivism (Vygotsky, 1962), and constructionism (e.g., Papert and Harel, 1991). Constructionism is a teaching philosophy and framework for learning and educative action (diSessa and Cobb, 2004) that builds upon Vygotsky's (1962) social constructivist theory and Piaget's constructivist theory. In constructionist learning, students engage in conscious construction of a technologically mediated computational artifact in a workshop-style group educational environment (Papert and Harel, 1991). This approach holds that individuals learn best when mobilizing their entire selves in a personally meaningful pursuit while sensing that their work is valued as part of a larger enterprise (Barron and Darling-Hammond, 2008; Stager 2001). Aligning with social constructivism, constructionist interventions are designed to facilitate learners' building of knowledge socially through dialogue and interaction, rather than by receiving it in a top-down way from a sole instructor and a print text. It adds computational creation of an artifact

TABLE 9.1

Knowledge-building.

Knowledge-building (Scardamalia, 2002)	
1.	**Real ideas and authentic problems.** In a classroom knowledge-building community, learners are concerned with understanding, based on real problems in the real world.
2.	**Improvable ideas.** Students' ideas are regarded as improvable objects.
3.	**Idea diversity.** In the classroom, the diversity of ideas raised by students is necessary.
4.	**Rise above.** Through a sustained improvement of ideas and understanding, students create higher-level concepts.
5.	**Epistemic agency.** Students themselves find their way in order to advance.
6.	**Community knowledge, collective responsibility.** Students' contribution to improving their collective knowledge in the classroom is the primary purpose of the knowledge-building classroom.
7.	**Democratizing knowledge.** All individuals are invited to contribute to the knowledge advancement in the classroom.
8.	**Symmetric knowledge advancement.** A goal for knowledge-building communities is to have individuals and organizations actively working to provide a reciprocal advance of their knowledge.
9.	**Pervasive knowledge-building.** All students contribute to collective knowledge-building.
10.	**Constructive uses of authoritative sources.** All members, including the teacher, sustain inquiry as a natural approach to support their understanding.
11.	**Knowledge-building discourse.** Students are engaged in discourse to share with each other, and to improve the knowledge advancement in the classroom.
12.	**Concurrent, embedded, and transformative assessment.** Students take a global view of their understanding, then decide how to approach their assessments. They create and engage in assessments in a variety of ways.

through programming as a key element. Overall, learning occurs through guided discovery—through peers' interactions with one another, material resources (in this case, an online LMS and software), a workshop-based in-person setting, and an expert mentor (Papert and Harel, 1991).

The literature on knowledge building (e.g., Scardamalia, 2002) is related to constructionism and is also a useful perspective to highlight, given its relevance to wikis for education. Knowledge building addresses how learning contexts can be designed to facilitate students' own building of theories and conceptual artifacts. A primary goal of this approach is to engage learners in sustained collaborative inquiry and to provide them with opportunities to work creatively with ideas (Chan, 2013). "Knowledge-sharing" has been distinguished from knowledge building in that knowledge sharing involves the flow of information and knowledge co-construction (development of shared understanding), whereas in knowledge building, the goal is to collaboratively construct *new ideas* through discourse, in resolution of authentic problems (Aalst, 2009). While in knowledge building the product of student collaborative engagement and discourse is often a conceptual artifact or set of ideas represented in speech or written documentation, in constructionism, the productive outcome comprises both conceptual *and* actual concrete computational artifacts, such as a game (Reynolds and Hmelo-Silver, 2013).

Scardamalia (2002) proposes twelve principles as conditions of knowledge-building interventions, presented in table 9.1. Linkages have been identified among these principles, to the conditions of constructionist interventions, and to the instructional design strategies employed in Globaloria (Reynolds and Hmelo-Silver, 2013). Overall, by involving students in a workshop-based blended learning classroom setting, and providing a host of wiki-based LMS resources, Globaloria aims to actualize the knowledge-building conditions described below in student learning.

WIKIS AS A LEARNING MANAGEMENT SYSTEM PLATFORM

As a form of participatory media, wikis can support student knowledge building, serving as both a point of shared reference and of shared production among students who engage freely in cultivating a base of online content. If designed to do so, such environments can add structure to student project-based work (e.g., creation of a digital artifact such as a game) by offering a host of pre-selected and pre-stocked, curated information resources, assignments, and activities. Salomon, Perkins and Globerson (1991) describe such a resource as a "coordinating representation"—a type of scaffolding support in which "an intelligent technology can undertake a significant part of the cognitive process that otherwise would have to be managed by the person." Among *undergraduates,* wikis have been found to be effective in supporting project-based work, making it easier for actors to work in parallel, multitask, and make "common sense" of the situation and how to proceed with the action (Larusson and Alterman, 2009, 375).

The wiki-based LMS in Globaloria serves this role as a coordinating representation for middle school and high school students, which is novel for this age group in the knowledge domain of computer science education and computational thinking. The design and deployment requires thoughtful planning to curate the resources, activities, and assignments, and to format the site navigation for students' optimal uses. However, once an initial implementation for a given course is developed, this implementation can be refined and iterated over many cycles as the course or module is retaught and the educator observes student experiences with it. Iterative design is a key principle.

In addition, the MediaWiki technology platform provides teachers with automatic reporting, allowing them to monitor and assess students' ongoing digital work activity, tracking site usage history, page edits, and file uploads. These auto-generated reports in the system can be coupled with the addition of GoogleAnalytics page read data options, facilitating evidence-based practice by educators who can pull reports and make adjustments to in-class scheduling and instruction on-the-fly given data results.

Globaloria Implementation of the Wiki-Based LMS

The figures below indicate ways in which the wiki-based LMS in Globaloria has been employed to support students' game design learning. Readers can adapt this model in support of their own students' digital project-based learning in schools.

Infrastructure. MediaWiki is the platform upon which Globaloria was built, which is a free server-based software open source wiki package written in PHP, originally for use on Wikipedia. It is now also used by several other projects of the nonprofit Wikimedia Foundation and by many other wikis, worldwide. Those who select MediaWiki as their solution will host the software and site content on their own servers. MediaWiki developer communities have created a large array of extensions that augment the core functionality. Several extensions have been employed in Globaloria to offer more advanced features and tools to augment the learner's experience. These include supports for a greater variety of file type uploading, user progress tracking, and expanded log-in permissions layer options.

Replication and Administration

The Globaloria game design curriculum, assignments, resources, and social media features have been created by a nonprofit organization that licenses out the material to its school partners, as part of a full suite of curriculum and professional development services. Partner schools are given their own replication of the game design course curriculum and all of its contents, as a pre-stocked course shell. Every school receives its own platform replication, as well as individual-level user accounts for administrators, teachers, and students that are created with permissions levels for the school only, so each school's material is password-protected and secure. Globaloria also features a shared teacher's hub wiki platform, in which teachers from the entire network of participating schools gain access to teaching resources such as grading rubrics, mentorship

Globaloria Course Offerings			
Course	**Time**	**Grade**	**Student Learning Goals**
Essentials of Game Design	25-35 hrs	4th and 5th	Practice basic digital literacy skills and learn to participate in a blended-learning class. Learn foundational concepts of game design, mechanics and coding.
Intro to Game Design (JavaScript)	40-55 hrs	6th and up	Learn fundamentals of game design and coding by creating a two-level game using HTML5 and JavaScript. Follow a real-world design and engineering process. (Fall 2015)
Intro to Game Design (ActionScript)	40-55 hrs	6th and up	Learn to code and design two games using Flash and ActionScript following a real-world design and engineering process.
Intro to 3D Game Design	40-55 hrs	9th and up	Learn to develop a 3D adventure game that is fun and educational using JavaScript and Unity.
Intermediate Game Design	40-55 hrs	6th and up	Deepen design, programming and teamwork skills. Collaboratively create a complex learning game using a professional process. Prerequisite: Intro to Game Design (ActionScript)
Mobile Game Design	40-55 hrs	6th and up	Learn to design and code a 2D game that leverages mobile-device features, like touch screen and smaller screen size. Export and test on mobile devices. Prerequisite: Intro to Game Design (ActionScript)

FIGURE 9.1

Globaloria game design course offerings.

protocols, schedules, organizers, and professional development activities. The Globaloria organization manages and updates the central platform, as well as the school, classroom, teacher and student member accounts and replications as a hosted solution for schools. Globaloria also offers extensive professional development support services to schools, teachers, and administrators who participate and sign on, including summer in-person training institutes and ongoing webinars for teacher education.

Game Design Curriculum. Figure 9.1 presents the variety of different Globaloria course offerings toward which the wiki-based LMS is adapted for use.

Wiki-Based LMS Content and Features

Students follow a sequence of activity units and course content. In the first half of the school year, units 1–3, they work individually and in the second half of the school year, units 4–6, the assignments move to teamwork. Student engagement in the latter phase becomes more self-paced, emergent, and open. During this time, teachers must differentiate instruction to help guide students and teams as they engage more in inquiry activity with the wiki LMS resources for learning to program and code.

The LMS contains three types of features:

1. Information resources including curriculum, assignments, schedules, syllabi, and in-depth video- and text-based tutorials for game design and programming.
2. Social media features including profile, project, and team pages that facilitate communication among classmates as well as collaboration through sharing and discussion of game assets.
3. Project management features enabling uploading, sharing, and archiving of in-progress and final game artifacts, which are uploaded as files and organized through varying structures on the site, including recommended versioning and file naming conventions.

Figures 9.2–9.5 demonstrate several of the instructional units of the game design curriculum through which students in Globaloria proceed. For a full-year implementation, there are a total of six units. During the first two units, working as individuals, students learn introductory programming by creating a simplified "hidden object game" which teaches some basic programming fundamentals. They then segue into teamwork in units 3–6, choosing a more complex game idea in a particular genre such as a platform jumper game, adventure game, or maze. Students are encouraged to develop game themes and a message through online research. At some locations, they may create a game about a particular school subject such as math.

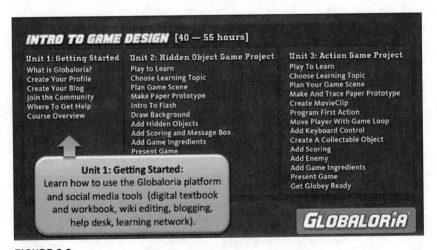

FIGURE 9.2

Examples of learning units for introduction to game design course, offered on the wiki LMS.

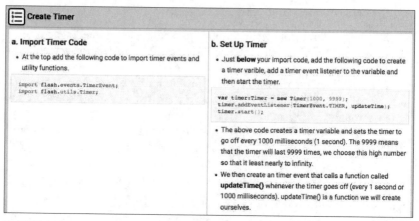

FIGURE 9.3
Screenshot example of curriculum page for programming tutorials.

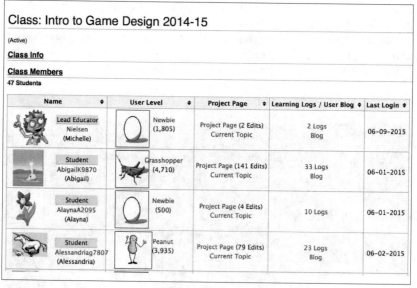

FIGURE 9.4
Screenshot example of class student directory, including links to student profile pages, project pages, learning logs, and blogs.

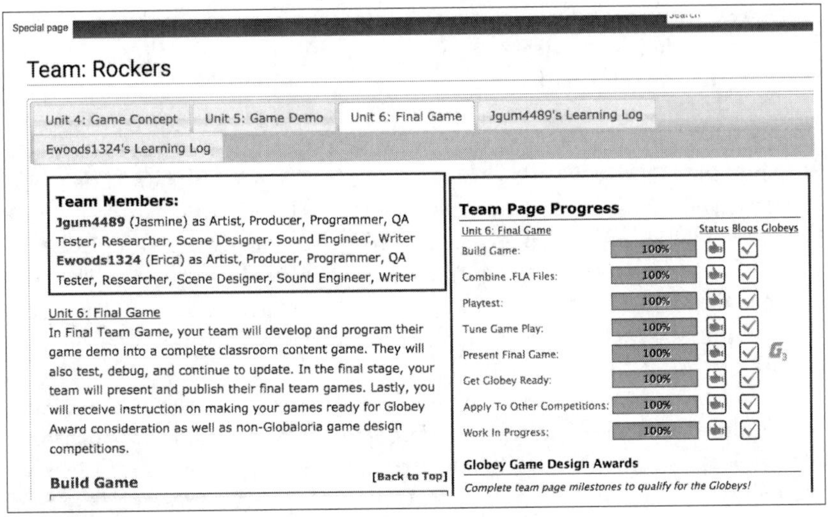

FIGURE 9.5
Screenshot example of game design project management features: team pages, where team members upload and manage game asset files and track their progress.

Research on Wiki LMS Uses

Here we describe some of the findings on differences in site usage among just two teams of students at a school in East Austin, Texas. The findings draw on click stream (Google Analytics) page read data from the wiki-based LMS for the 2012/2013 school year. We report *only the two case study schools,* which we are labeling "ARCPA" (middle school [MS] only) and "ARCPA2" (middle school and high school [HS] students). The data represents user page view actions from a total of 211 ARCPA MS students, and 437 ARCPA2 MS/HS students. At ARCPA2 there were more MS students (332) than HS students (105) and thus the majority of the data set reflects students in grades 6–8. These students participated in game design daily, for credit and a grade for the entire school year.

Google Analytics data are available at the school-level in aggregate for the whole wiki platform being used by a given school. Across these locations, ARCPA students created a total of 142 hidden object games and ARCPA2 students created a total of 288 hidden object games, which are the culmination of preliminary introductory activity for curriculum units entitled "Intro," "Units 1," and "Unit 2." Students at ARCPA created a total of 50 full final team games, and ARCPA2 students created a total of 83 team games, drawing upon curriculum units entitled "Unit 3" and "Unit 4." Further, throughout the time frame, students used the wiki-based LMS to support their game design and creation.

Every page on the Globaloria wiki LMS is mined by Google Analytics. Here we highlight page view data for the two primary sets of LMS features: social media and information resources.

Social Media Features. Profile pages are those pages editable by students, on which students post images and information about themselves to create an initial online identity. Profile pages do not contain game files or game work. *Project* pages are those pages editable by students, on which students post their individual-level hidden object game files and game design work from the first half of the school year. In contrast, *team* pages are those pages editable by all members of student teams, which serve as the locus of team activity, where they post shared game files, design plans, and text-based communications and discussions about the ongoing progress of their game.

Information Resources. Curriculum unit pages are not editable by students, and contain curriculum content, assignments, tutorials, and informational copy, video, and sample code to support game design learning. They include the following units: Intro, Wiki Tools, Units 1–4, and Actionscript Tutorials. Note that since our research data stem from the 2012/2013 school year, at that time, the curriculum was broken up into 4 units only (which was iterated and changed to 6 units for the present school year, as shown in the previous screenshots). Each of the four units contains at least five URLs of curriculum resources. The Wiki Tools area also includes the Game Gallery where students can view others' final playable games from previous years.

Analysis. Page view reports were run by school, in aggregate, and across the five time increments below. We exported the data from Google Analytics as Excel files, merging them into a master spreadsheet. We calculated standardized metrics, dividing total page views by the N of students at that location, to give a metric of average page views per student per year for the given resource. Some students participated for half a year and others for a full year, thus when we "standardized" our data, half-year students were counted as .5 whereas full-year students were counted as 1, thus our standardization procedure accounts for this time difference in the denominator.

RESULTS

Social Media Features

As a "coordinating representation," the wiki LMS helps students orient and make sense of their game design activity. The profile, project and team pages are the locus for coordinating students' active design and programming work, and where they archive, present, and share code. Profile pages are used early in the curriculum to establish their online identity; project and team pages relate more to actual game design and represent more substantive game design activity that occurs in programming software such as Flash or Unity.

TABLE 9.2

Descriptive data, standardized page views for social media pages
(average page views/student/year).

	Standardized profile page views	Standardized project page views	Standardized team page views
ARCPA	1969.08	325.01	59.00
ARCPA2	1016.05	54.06	96.06
Mean	**1493.15**	**189.85**	**77.08**

The locus of team engagement and activity is the team page. Here, they post game asset files including graphics as well as code, and they describe different pieces of their game. The profile, project, and team page frequency distribution for standardized page views, as well as their mean, are provided for each school in table 9.2 (i.e., average page views *per student,* across the entire school year).

These page view findings indicate that on the whole, students visited their profile pages more so than the more productivity-oriented project pages or team pages across this school year. It appears that ARCPA students viewed profile and project pages substantially more on average than ARCPA2 students, whereas ARCPA2 students viewed team pages more. Cross-time uses are shown in figures 9.6–9.8. Note that the page view scales vary in each figure, and these metrics are average page views *per student.*

In these cross-time tables, we see that at both schools, profile page views occurred more in the earlier phases of the curriculum, whereas project page views occur in the second time frame, and team page views occurred more in

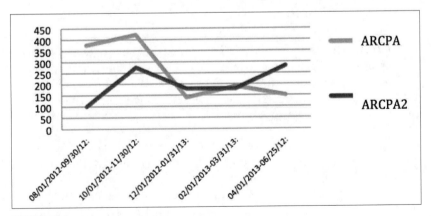

FIGURE 9.6

Profile page views across time.

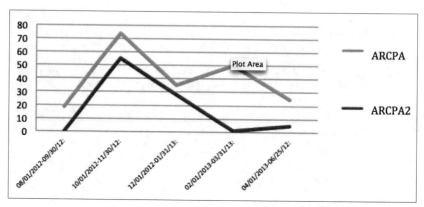

FIGURE 9.7
Project page views across time.

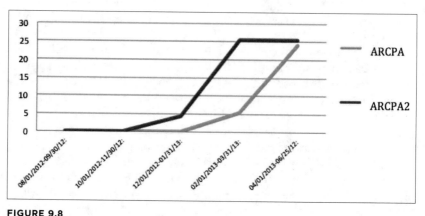

FIGURE 9.8
Team page views across time.

the fourth and fifth. Students at ARCPA2 viewed the team pages about equally on average in both latter time frames, and more overall. The team page serves as a location to organize, structure, and showcase file attributes, reflecting a modular approach to completing the game artifact. Page view data here indicate that students do not appear to arrive at team page uses until quite late in the curriculum.

Information Resource Use Features. Non-editable curricular unit pages contain information necessary for student game design. Findings indicate that at both schools, students appear to engage much more with topics residing earlier in the curriculum sequence (Intro, Wiki Tools, unit 1, unit 2) than later (units 3, 4, Actionscript Tutorials) on average. The frequency distribution for standardized page views (i.e., average page views per student across the entire

TABLE 9.3
Descriptive data, standardized page views for information resource features (average page views/student/year).

	Intro	Wiki Tools	Unit 1	Unit 2	Unit 3	Unit 4	Actionscript Tutorials
ARCPA	890.01	367.09	20.09	97.09	62.06	1.03	42.07
ARCPA2	86.04	133.04	8.05	48.02	25.03	0.09	21.01
Mean	**488.25**	**250.65**	**14.07**	**73.05**	**43.95**	**1.01**	**31.09**

school year) for the curriculum pages are presented in table 9.3. Findings across time by school are displayed in figures 9.9 and 9.10 below.

In the cross-time figures, the charts are on the same scale. We see that the two schools appear to vary substantially in their informational page views in both patterns and frequencies. ARCPA students overall appear to have utilized the wiki LMS curriculum substantially more than students at ARCPA2. It is important to note that these standardized data at the school level of analysis render opaque the nuances of team- and individual-level variation in activity.

Inferences Based on Context Differences. The game design program at ARCPA was much more established than at ARCPA2 by the time these data

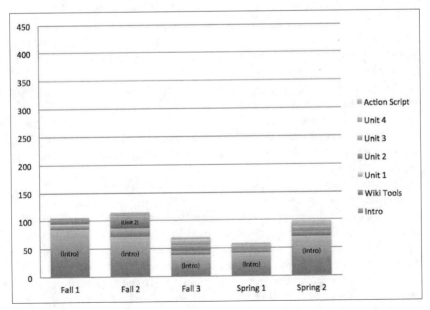

FIGURE 9.9
ARCPA curriculum unit page views across time.

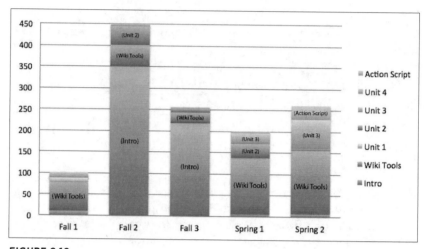

FIGURE 9.10

ARCPA2 curriculum unit page views across time.

were aggregated. Students in middle school at ARCPA take the class daily, for credit and a grade, and many of the students take the class for three years in a row during middle school, advancing in the depth and breadth of their expertise each year as they retake the class and develop more complex games. At ARCPA, the program had already been in place for three years by this 2012/2013 school year. Thus, the 8th grade cohort at ARCPA was in their third year of engagement. The 7th grade cohort was in their second year and the 6th grade cohort was in their first year.

In contrast, at ARCPA2, the 2012/2013 school year was the second year of the program, and only one small class of students had taken it in the first year, thus for the majority of students it was their first year of participation. The differences seen could be partially explained by ARCPA students' prior experience and familiarity with the LMS resources, and thus greater capacity for autonomous engagement.

Further, anecdotally the researcher observed substantially different teaching styles between the ARCPA and ARCPA2 educators. At ARCPA, there were two educators who were also both in their third year of teaching Globaloria. Both had largely embraced offering an autonomous learning climate in their classrooms that encouraged independent student work. By this third year, the teachers at ARCPA were observed to offer much less frequent top-down instruction at the Smart Board, instead circulating to monitor students, especially those in 8th grade (and notably, there were no 8th grade participants at ARCPA2). ARCPA teachers spent individual time with any new arrivals to the program, but also paired new arrivals with advanced students, encouraging peer learning.

In contrast, the most active teacher at ARCPA2, who taught the vast majority of students in several different classes, employed a much tighter managerial style in the classroom. Students in her classes all proceeded through the same set of activities at the same time, and she often waited for the whole class to finish a scheduled assignment before moving everyone on to the next curriculum phase. She offered top-down instruction daily. This approach kept the class more organized and consistent, but this may have held more advanced students back somewhat from independently exploring and utilizing the resources provided.

The findings above indicate that ARCPA2 shows evidence of fairly consistent uses of the wiki curriculum across time. At ARCPA, we see more sweeping variation in the curriculum uses, where the teachers encouraged students to work at their own pace. For students who were driven to do so, this approach appeared to support their movement into unit 3 and the Actionscript tutorials at the latter phases. We also see that the page views to the Wiki Tools are fairly substantial in the latter two curriculum units for ARCPA. Deeper analysis at the URL level shows that ARCPA students much more substantially utilized the File Uploader feature in the latter phases. This indicates that students were quite active at ARCPA in creating, uploading, archiving, and cataloging many game files on the site. The ARCPA2 students, in contrast, were all given thumb drives for sharing and transferring files across computers, which means that some may not have used this file transfer affordance in the same way.

Overall, these data provide an anchor for considering variations in program implementation factors at different locations, and the opportunities and challenges of using page view activity to research (and even evaluate and assess) patterns of engagement across schools.

DISCUSSION

The use of Google Analytics page-read data in construct with deployment of a wiki LMS as a coordinating representation for student project-based work can facilitate educator monitoring, evaluation, and assessment of students' learning. For instance, it might have come as a surprise to educators that students were not accessing their team pages earlier, had they themselves been tracking this data on a real-time basis. Similarly, educators may have a goal for students to be actively engaging in use of a particular curriculum tutorial, and real-time web metrics can let them know the extent to which their students are doing so. Overall, in the Globaloria context, the findings at ARCPA and ARCPA2 also indicate that some teachers may need further professional development to better understand how to support student uses of the available wiki resources for game design learning.

One key limitation in interpretation is that the data are available at the page level of analysis only (not by member ID), thus the page metrics presented are class aggregates. However, if teachers create a curriculum in which students are required to build their own self-named projects pages (which will each get a unique URL that can be tracked), and post content and files to these pages continuously, the web metrics can allow the teacher to assess student engagement in project-based work at the individual level, too.

The standard Google Analytics account type is free. Google offers guidelines and instructions online for implementing their tracking script. The data reporting in the free version includes page visits, referral URL data (what page a given visitor was on just prior to visiting the given URL), average time spent on the page, and repeat visitation. The reporting tool also enables batching of reports into time increments (e.g., how did page views to a given URL change across weeks). The script can be implemented within wiki code, so long as the author can edit the HTML of a given wiki page, and add the required Google Analytics script, which will look similar to the code depicted in figure 9.11. Most wiki software enables this editing.

Figure 9.12 shows a screenshot sample of the standard reporting dashboard in the free version of the Google Analytics tool.

In addition to Google Analytics page reads, many wikis offer "trace log data reporting" of site activity as a feature of the platform itself, which includes native metrics on page edits and file uploads through the wiki history. In some cases, these data are available to site administrators at the individual student member level of analysis, which will allow teachers to track their students' editing and uploading activity in the LMS across time. Usually this requires that students must log in first before editing, which is often set as the default administrative permissions modality.

```
<script type="text/javascript">

var_gaq=_gaq || □;
_gaq.push(['_setAccount','UA-37160931-1']);
_gaq.push(['_trackPageview']);

(function(){
var ga = document.createElement("script"); ga.type = "text/javascript"; ga.async = true;
ga.src = ("https." == document.location.protocol ? "https://ssl':'http://www') + '.google-analytics.
com/ga.js'; var s = document.getElementsByTagName('script')[0]; s.parentNode.insertBefore(ga, s);
})();

</script>
```

FIGURE 9.11

Sample Google Analytics web metrics tracking script.

The use of site metrics to monitor student engagement is important for educators because the extent to which certain students are (or are not) utilizing the learning resources provided may not be evident from one's classroom observation. Educators may be surprised at the level of engagement of some students. The Globaloria research case study data shows several instances of this phenomenon. A student who is typically reserved in the classroom may appear as inactive observationally, and may be downgraded for participation. However, that student may be engaging actively in uses of the resources, learning, and development of artifacts. Recognition of such solo activity might be lost in the context of an emphasis on teamwork in situ. Further, some team members might be significantly more active than others in their actual digital creation productivity, which might not be as evident in observing students' classroom behavior and dialogue. Wiki site metrics can help educators to better understand these dynamics, intervene to offer greater supports to less active students, and overall, evaluate students more appropriately.

The types of assessment can include rubrics of activity customized to accommodate known appropriate levels or thresholds of relative page views and/or wiki edits and uploads. Educators can develop spreadsheets to observe class averages. Google Analytics offers Excel exports for all results at the URL level. Wiki metrics can be transposed from HTML into Excel fairly easily. Educators may want to gauge student activity in real time, look at highs, lows, and averages, and consider where individuals fall within the total class range for the use of a given resource or engagement with a given editable page.

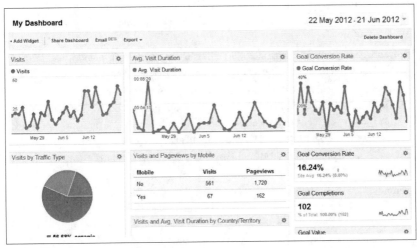

FIGURE 9.12
Sample Google Analytics reporting dashboard.

The use of data in educational decision making is expected throughout the education system—from the federal to the state, district, school, and classroom levels (Means et al., 2009). As learning management systems and web service environments such as wikis continue to expand into broader use, educators must continue to evolve their data-driven decision making, appropriating new site metrics capabilities that web-based platforms afford. This chapter offers an exemplar for both implementing a wiki for students' project-based learning, and educator assessment of student engagement in such a platform. The aim is to spark educators' motivation and interest in leveraging these environments as "coordinating representations" to support student cognition and metacognition, and their knowledge building while engaging in blended learning as a formal in-school educational experience.

REFERENCES

Aalst, Jan Van. 2009. "Distinguishing Knowledge-Sharing, Knowledge-Construction, and Knowledge-Creation Discourses." *International Journal of Computer-Supported Collaborative Learning Computer Supported Learning* 4, no. 3: 259–87.

Barron, B., and L. Darling-Hammond, 2008. "Teaching for Meaningful Learning: A Review of Research on Inquiry-Based and Cooperative Learning." www.edutopia.org/pdfs/edutopia-teaching-for-meaningful-learning.pdf.

Chan, C. K. K. 2013. "Collaborative Knowledge-Building: Towards a Knowledge Creation Perspective." In *International Handbook of Collaborative Learning*, ed. C. E. Hmelo-Silver, C. A. Chinn, C. K. K. Chan, and A. M. O'Donnell, 437–61. New York: Taylor and Francis.

diSessa, Andrea A., and Paul Cobb. 2004. "Ontological Innovation and the Role of Theory in Design Experiments." *Journal of the Learning Sciences* 13, no. 1: 77–103.

Larusson, J. A., and R. Alterman. 2009. "Wikis to Support the "Collaborative" Part of Collaborative Learning." *Computer-Supported Collaborative Learning*, 4: 371–402.

Means, B., C. Padilla, A. DeBarger, and M. Bakia. 2009. "Implementing Data-Informed Decision Making in Schools: Teacher Access, Supports and Use." Report prepared for U.S. Department of Education, Office of Planning, Evaluation and Policy Development by SRI International, Menlo Park, CA.

Papert, S., and I. Harel, eds. 1991. *Constructionism: Research Reports and Essays, 1985–1990.* Norwood, NJ: Ablex.

Reynolds, R., and C. Hmelo-Silver. 2013. "Areas of Theoretical Convergence in the Globaloria Game Design Initiative: Constructionism, Knowledge-Building and Guided Discovery-Based Learning." Paper presented at the American Education Research Association, San Francisco, CA, April.

Salomon, G., D. Perkins, and T. Globerson. 1991. "Partners in Cognition: Extending Human Intelligence with Intelligent Technologies." *Educational Researcher* 20, no. 3: 2–9.

Scardamalia, M. 2002. "Collective Cognitive Responsibility for the Advancement of Knowledge." In *Liberal Education in a Knowledge Society*, ed. B. Smith, 67–98. Chicago: Open Court.

Stager, G. 2001. "Computationally-Rich Constructionism and At-Risk Learners." Paper presented at the 2001 World Conference on Computers in Education. Copenhagen, Denmark. www.stager.org/wcce/index.html.

Vygotsky, L. S. 1962. *Thought and Language*. Cambridge, MA: MIT Press.

ALEXANDER KÖNIG
AND JAN HODEL

10
Wikis in History Education at the Upper Secondary Level

WIKIS CAN BE USED IN THE TEACHING OF HISTORY IN MANY ways. There are three aspects of learning history: exploring the writing of history, the joint examination of history, and the role of media in learning history. These aspects show the specific potential of applying wikis to history classes, which is seldom discussed in the didactics of history.[1] Overall, wikis open up new and diverse opportunities to formulate subject-specific learning environments, which can be set up in a collaborative and procedural manner. These educational technologies can especially help the teachers to initiate and consolidate the learning processes of history. The following examples show how the use of wikis can enhance a teacher's methodological repertoire, where wikis facilitate the development of more individualized and differentiated learning opportunities.

The writing of history is indeed widely discussed as important in the didactics of history, but it is still rarely applied in the classroom. The practice of group work is maintained and regularly used in the teaching of history, though its importance for history learning is rarely discussed in detail (see also Hodel and Waldis, 2007). The combination of these two approaches in the collaborative writing of history is a form of examining history which appears promising and is made possible by the new digital tools such as wiki technology. However, there exists little experience of such applications. On the other hand, the possibilities of new media technologies raise the fundamental question of how history can be collaboratively learned and recorded, as well as how the media characterizes the learning of history as a learning environment (and not as a learning object or learning tool) (Bernsen, König, and Spahn, 2012).

The following two concrete examples outline the opportunities and challenges of the use of wikis in history classes. The experiences are drawn from the lesson units developed and implemented in the advanced history course at the Theodor-Heuss-Gymnasium in Sulzbach (Saar, Germany). The wiki software MediaWiki was used, which operates using the same engine as Wikipedia. In the following teaching scenarios, the students were not only able to try out the collaborative examination of history using an online tool, but also got to know the functions of a well-known online encyclopedia. The wiki work was integrated into the methodology of conventional classes and lesson units (Meyer, 1994, 38).

Context of the Lesson Unit

Subject: History

School year: 2006/07

Class level: College level (grade 12/13)[2]

Number of students in class: 15 students

School type: Secondary school

Number of lesson hours: 2 hours (example 1); 4 hours (example 2)

Participating teacher: Alexander König (History teacher)

EXAMPLE 1
COLLABORATIVE INTERPRETATION
OF SOURCES AND RECONSTRUCTION OF HISTORY

The students are confronted with various kinds of media during their schooling. In history lessons, sources and illustrations are investigated, appropriate methodologies are explained, and the acquired action knowledge is practiced (Sauer and Fleiter, 2003). In this arrangement, the technical possibilities of software can help the students to acquire the skills of writing hypertexts and collaborating in the digital medium. Moreover, in terms of methodology, they can develop skills and capabilities in re- and de-construction (König, 2010), which can be summarized as historical online competences in the digital medium (reading, writing, and speaking/reflection) (Hodel, 2007; Hodel, 2008).

The focus of this lesson, however, was the subject-specific handling of various kinds of sources. In the corresponding topic "USA—a country on the path to world power," the students worked using different image sources. Among them were two cartoons portraying American foreign policies in the twentieth century. These cartoons were provided on two otherwise empty pages in a MediaWiki. The class was divided into two equal teams, each of which had to work on a cartoon. Smaller groups with a maximum of three people were formed within each team, and the teams were provided with computers for the task.

Since the software did not allow simultaneous editing of the same page (see "Example 2" below), the students in their groups were assigned one of the following consecutive tasks:

- Describe the cartoon.
- Explain its historical background.
- Interpret the symbols and clarify the author's intention.

The students were instructed to insert a heading for each step of the editing using the software (including a description, historical background, and meanings), and the chapter thus created on the wiki page could be worked on as a single element of the page without the risk of repetitions.

The complete lesson sequence went through three phases until the entire source analysis was complete. Each step took about eight minutes. A group began with the assigned task, such as the description (phase 1). After that, the group switched to working on a document from another group (e.g., the historical background) and took over the editing work of the previous group. The students were expected to read and evaluate the work, to make changes and improvements if necessary (phase 2), and finally continue with the next step (e.g., interpretation). As a whole, the arrangement was comparable to a digital group puzzle. In various stages, the groups engage intensively with certain aspects of the material in relation to factual and value judgments, as well as with the viewpoints developed by other groups.

In the second hour of the lesson, both cartoons were addressed by all the students. At the same time, the teachers gave the students the opportunity to share their experience of the wiki work. The students were finally given a task to read and possibly improve the current analysis again as homework. Interestingly, some students expanded the current hypertexts on their own, so that individual aspects of the newly generated wiki pages were deepened in content.

EXAMPLE 2
VIRTUAL PREPARATION FOR HISTORY LEARNING OUTSIDE THE SCHOOL

In the second example, students learned about the Battle of Verdun, which is considered the epitome of a battle of attrition. The wiki was used in this example to prepare the students for an excursion to the historic site.

At the beginning of the lesson, the teacher introduced an advance organizer (Wahl, 2006, 139ff.), who gave the class a thematic overview. The students were then asked to perform tasks on the computer in pairs. Each group received a number of aspects (places, people, terms, etc.), on which they should gather information from textbooks and the Internet and write a short article. The students were then asked to improve the articles from other groups if necessary. On another wiki page, which was set up by the teacher, the students were asked to submit questions they thought of when reading the texts.

In both phases, time management was of great importance. The editing of the texts must be asynchronous due to the technical framework of the wiki used to prevent accidental repetitions through simultaneous editing. Therefore, the teacher asked the groups, for example, to post the questions during the working phase one after the other. The session began with the groups reading the article (for about five minutes) and making notes on each paper. Then the first group was asked to start editing (for five minutes), while the other groups would read the formulated texts and write comments on the paper. After that, the second group would proceed to edit the text.

This sequence was continued until the end of the hour, in order to ensure that only one group was in the edit mode on the wiki. As homework, the students were asked to read all outstanding texts and formulate more questions at home.

It was planned initially that the questions from the students would be made available to the historian during the course of the excursion, and his answers would be recorded. However, during the preparation, it was agreed that the expert could prepare his answers based on the questions raised on the wiki and answer them on the trip. Thus, the students were able to conduct an interview with the expert at the historic site, and record this with a camcorder and digital camera. They then processed the data and presented the resulting audiovisual file using the EmbedVideo extension on the wiki platform.

POTENTIALS FOR HISTORY EDUCATION AND FOR LEARNING WITH DIGITAL MEDIA

The introduction of wikis in the previous examples had a methodological aspect. The wiki was limited to individual lessons and teacher sequences that were included as blended-learning episodes of the course. To estimate the potential of wikis, the media education-didactic model (Baacke, 2007; Döbeli Honegger, 2007, 39ff.) of functional dependence on history didactics should be considered (Rohlfes, 1999, 18).

The lesson in the first example highlighted the collaborative reconstruction of history by co-writing a text. Historical representations always follow a pattern that incorporates individual statements with respect to the time horizon in a meaningful textual connection. In this present case, the students created a "re-narration," according to the terminology of Pandel (Pandel, 2010, 156–57). The materials handled by the students were unknown to them, but thanks to the knowledge acquired, they could put the information in a narrative context.

For this, the students also used source-critical methods, albeit in a simplified form. The teaching of source-critical methods was the second objective of the lesson.

Wiki technology functioned as a tool and a learning environment, in which the source analysis and the creation of narration were carried out cooperatively. The use of a wiki allowed a direct examination of the interpretations from different classmates. In this way, history could be experienced as a communicative and discursive structured negotiation of competitive interpretations. On the other hand, at least in this example, the creation of a hypertext along with the related possibilities of contextualization and detailing of reported facts took a back seat.

The task of the students in the second example can be referred to as a collaborative retelling (Pandel, 2010, 154ff.) of representations of history that already exist on the Internet. This narrative mode typically results in a reproduction of non-critical traditional thinking, but with the help of wiki technology, it was made fruitful use of by the students as a basis for formulating questions.

Consequently, the wiki acted both as a mini-lexicon, in which historical articles from different sources outside the school were collected, as well as a repository of questions from the students. Digital tools such as wiki technology show the new possibilities for learning and recording history in a collaborative manner, and they also lead to some fundamental considerations, such as the uses of media as a learning environment (and not only as learning objects or learning tools).

CONCLUSION:
WIKI WORK IN HISTORY HAS TO BE LEARNED!

In summary, the observations from the use of wikis confirm that the writing of history is not simply the textualization of knowledge, but is rather a part of the cognitive process itself. The collaborative writing of a wiki text stating historical facts proved to be a demanding task both in terms of content and technology, as well as in terms of methodology. The collaborative work on a wiki was an unusual and new experience for the students. In this regard, the teaching experience also confirms the empirical data, which shows that for overall Web 2.0 usage, collaborative writings such as Wikipedia find themselves in the second-to-last place with 1 percent of the data.

It would be wrong to interpret these numbers as a fundamental rejection of wikis. Young people are not reluctant to work with wikis. However, history learning requires specific online competences in the areas of reading, writing, speaking, and communication in regard to a wiki. The writing and collaborations on a wiki platform have to be learned and practiced!

Specifically, three practical difficulties are recognized while working with wikis, and they are important for the use of wikis in educational contexts:

- The students repeat the texts from other classmates unintentionally.[3]
- They also show a hesitation to edit the work of other classmates.
- The Wiki syntax was not well known to them, and despite the help of an editor, the wiki syntax proved to be not self-explanatory. A handout with a quick-start guide would have been useful.

Nevertheless, the students expressed a positive attitude to working with wikis. They have learned a lot about Wikipedia and the functioning of wikis as a whole. It was amazing for them to see how something could be published so easily on the Internet. One student described the process of source interpretation as "interesting." From his perspective, the analysis had shown in retrospect to be an important part of the "course work," by which means the students could develop source interpretations without further intervention by the teacher.

Based on the observation of the class, it can be said that the group discussions were intense before the writing of texts began. The texts were also written with care and consideration.[4]

Active and relatively independent learning came to the fore, while there was a change in the role of the teachers. The teacher became no longer a person who tells history, but a constructor of a web-based learning environment who stimulates the learning process in "the universe of history" (Gautschi, 2009, 43). The teacher's activities in the classroom were limited to consultation, facilitation, and troubleshooting. Here, the organization and the design of switching between online and offline phases played a significant role in the proper facilitation of history lessons.

The examples set out in the use of wikis for history lessons also show that the students with a good performance in class often performed well in text production too. They appeared to be "power users," delivering the majority of the texts and making changes to improve the text quality, while sharing their knowledge at the same time. The low-performing students could perform additional tasks such as formulating questions or giving descriptions to image sources.

It is noticeable that the students seldom made use of the opportunity to comment and discuss the work results, despite the provision of a discussion page for each document in the wiki. There are several possible explanations for this. On one hand, the face-to-face environment in a classroom allows the students to share and discuss their views and opinions directly. On the other hand are the aforementioned reservations to change or criticize the work of other students. However, the task given to the students did not explicitly require the use of the discussion pages.

These findings demonstrate the importance of well-formulated history learning tasks along with the use of digital media for teaching history. Should the wiki be able to contribute to a new working culture, both the technical aspects and didactic considerations on the internal differentiation (through individualization) need to be taken into account (Heuer, 2011).

NOTES

1. It would be the task of the "digital didactics of history" to establish the theoretical opportunities and challenges of collaborative writing tools, to investigate these empirically, and to develop them on a pragmatic level. This is so far a desideratum of research.

2. In Saarland, every grade 13 student of the advanced course had to take the central examination (*Abitur*), which lasts from three to five hours.

3. New technologies or work/learning environments (e.g., Google Docs, Etherpad) allow for synchronous editing of texts, which also show new perspectives for the collaborative creation of texts. On the other hand, these tools have limited possibilities to create simple hypertexts with modules linked to one another.

4. In an essay, Wolfgang Schmale suggests that digital encoding can be phenomenologically understood as an act of realization (Schmale, 2010, 13). It would be interesting to empirically test the extent to which students actually understand the work on the screen as an objectification of their thoughts. The controversial discussions that the groups led in front of the computer, as well as their struggle to formulate a consensus, is an indicator of this in anycase.

INTERNET REFERENCES

Wiki des Theodor-Heuss-Gymnasiums. 2011. Online: www.netzgymnasium.de/Wiki/index. php?title=Hauptseite.

REFERENCES

Baacke, D. 2007. *Medienpädagogik*. Tübingen: Max Niemayer Verlag.

Bernsen, D., A. König, and T. Spahn. 2012. "Medien und historisches Lernen: Eine Verhältnisbestimmung und ein Plädoyer für eine digitale Geschichtsdidaktik." *Zeitschrift für digitale Geschichtswissenschaften* 1, no. 1. http://universaar .unisaarland.de/journals/index.php/zdg/article/view/294/358.

Döbeli Honegger, B. 2007. "Wikis und die starken Potentiale: Unterrichten mit Wikis als virtuellen Wandtafeln." *Computer + Unterricht* 17, no. 66: 39–41.

Gautschi, P. 2009. *Guter Geschichtsunterricht: Grundlagen, Erkenntnisse, Hinweise*. Schwalbach: Wochenschau-Verlag.

Heuer, C. 2011. "Gütekriterien für kompetenzorientierte Lernaufgaben im Fach Geschichte." *Geschichte in Wissenschaft und Unterricht* 62, nos. 7/8: 443–55.

Hinze, U., M. Bischoff, and G. Blakowski. 2002. "Jigsaw Method in the Context of CSCL." http://home.arcor.de/udo-hinze/Dokumente/Jigsaw.pdf.

Hodel, J. 2007. "Historische Online-Kompetenz. Informations und Kommunikationstechnologie in den Geschichtswissenschaften." In *Geschichte lehren an der Hochschule: Bestandsaufnahme, methodische Ansätze, Perspektiven*, ed. R. Pöppinghege, 194–210. Schwalbach: Wochenschau-Verlag.

———. 2008. "Digital lesen, digital schreiben, digital denken? Über den kompetenten Umgang mit Geschichte im Zeitalter des digitalen Medienwandels." In *Am Anfang ist das Wort: Lexika in der Schweiz*, ed. M. Jorio and C. Eggs, 113–25. Baden: Verlag hier und jetzt.

Hodel, J., and M. Waldis. 2007. "Sichtstrukturen im Geschichtsunterricht—die Ergebnisse der Videoanalyse." In *Geschichtsunterricht heute: Eine empirische Analyse ausgewählter Aspekte*, ed. P. Gautschi et al., 91–142. Bern: hep verlag ag.

König, A. 2007. *Wikis im Geschichtsunterricht*. www.lehrer-online.de/wiki-ge -schichte.php.

———. 2008a. "Die Schlacht von Verdun: Unterrichtspraktische Erfahrungen zu selbstorganisiertem Lernen mit Wikis im Geschichtsunterricht." *Computer + Unterricht* 18, no. 69: 25–27.

———. 2008b. "Kollaborative Quelleninterpretation mit Wikis." *Didaktische Handlungsmöglichkeiten und methodische Gestaltungsfelder im Geschichtsunterricht* 2.0. *Login* 28, no. 162: 47–52.

———. 2010. "Geschichte mit digitalen Medien re- und dekonstruieren: Kompetenzorientiertes historisches Lernen im computer- und webgestützten Geschichtsunterricht." *Computer + Unterricht* 20, no. 77: 26–32.

Magenheim, J. 2004. "CSCL in der Schule." In *CSCL-Kompendium: Lehr- und Handbuch zum computerunterstützten kooperativen Lernen*, ed. J. Haake, G. Schwabe, and M. Wessner, 358–69. Munich: Oldenbourg Wissenschaftsverlag.

Medienpädagogischer Forschungsverbund Südwest, ed. 2010. *JIM-Studie 2010: Jugend, Information, (Multi-)Media: Basisuntersuchung zum Medienumgang 12- bis 19-Jähriger in Deutschland.* Stuttgart: Medienpädagogischer Forschungsverbund Südwest.

Meyer, H. 1994. *UnterrichtsMethoden,* vol. 1: *Theorieband.* 6th edition. Berlin: Cornelsen Verlag Scriptor.

Pandel, H. 2010. *Historisches Erzählen: Narrativität im Geschichtsunterricht.* Schwalbach: Wochenschau-Verlag.

Rohlfes, J. 1999. "Geschichtsdidaktik: Geschichte, Begriff, Gegenstand." In *Geschichtsunterricht heute: Grundlagen, Probleme, Möglichkeiten,* ed. M. Sauer, 18–21. Seelze-Velber: Friedrich Verlag.

Sauer, M., and E. Fleiter. 2003. *Lernbox Geschichte: Das Methodenbuch.* 2nd edition. Seelze-Velber: Friedrich Verlag.

Schmale, W. 2010. *Digitale Geschichtswissenschaft.* Vienna: Böhlau Verlag.

Wahl, D. 2006. *Lernumgebungen erfolgreich gestalten: Vom trägen Wissen zum kompetenten Handeln.* 2nd enlarged edition. Bad Heilbrunn: Julius Klinkhardt Verlag.

BEAT KNAUS

11

The Use of Wikis in German Secondary School Teaching

THE BASIC IDEA BEHIND A WIKI IS, IN ESSENCE, STILL UNDER-conceptualized. Like many groundbreaking inventions before, it is used very keenly, but its dimensions are not yet articulated. The term *wiki* means more than the eponymous encyclopedia; it represents a radical new process of writing and generating knowledge through writing for the vision of collaborative creation which has become a reality. The wiki can readily support human knowledge generation. Wiki functionality invites reimagining fundamental terms from Western intellectual history, such as "author," "text," "read," and "write." The author resigns as the sole creator of the text; instead the authorship is taken by a collective that can continuously expand and renew itself. In principle, the text is also never completed; but rather it always continues to be written, updated, and linked. And finally, the reading process is no longer the blind retracing of a completed product, but essentially the first step in its optimization.

THE BENEFITS

Secondary schools, as one custodian of knowledge, must skeptically face such literally[1] fast-paced revolutions, and will not remain unaffected. Wikis will set a precedent, even in secondary school, and most visibly in German classes. As much as the implications of carelessly using the encyclopedia are undesirable, all of the synergy effects, which result from the controlled use of wikis in a performance and student-oriented German class at secondary school, are equally desirable:

1. The vision of a fluid text becomes a reality with wiki: instead of an erratic block, which seemingly appears from nowhere in a singular act of manual text creation, a text form is used, which is recognizable as a semi-finished product from the outset with its need for revision. Thus, a process-oriented writing technique, which is postulated in German didactics,[2] is institutionalized by itself, so to speak, through the choice of the medium.

2. Wikis as a medium to facilitate teaching German have a positive effect on the motivation of the learners. They serve as a kind of Trojan horse: while computer technology is integrated into the curriculum with its great identification potential for young people, it is possible to transport content which is normally met with less acceptance with regard to conventional teaching methods.

3. In wiki practice, the ICT and media literacy required by many secondary school curricula are no more buzzwords than an inconvenient additional learning objective. The question of the advantages and disadvantages of medialization for schools answers itself through the natural use of source texts, dealing with development and preparation issues, and presenting and publishing knowledge.

4. When the class utilizes a wiki, the position of the teacher is relativized in a wholesome manner. Instead of being the first and for the most part only authority on texts, which they officially have to judge, they become an equal reader among many who provide support with regard to the written texts on their way into the public domain. Indeed, they lose their sphinxlike aura as sole critic, but they gain much more natural authority as first among equals.

THE REQUIREMENTS

For wikis to function smoothly in secondary school German classes, it is recommended to follow the maxim *Keep it short and simple* (KISS), which was originally used in information technology. This begins with the allocation of rights: in principle, all users of the system, regardless of whether they are teachers or learners, owners of the document or editors of the document, should have equal rights. As is generally known, all well-known wiki variants have a version history, a fallback system which allows you to undo any mistakes or abuse at any time. Willful breaches of rules rarely occur in practice: it is a strong sign for the teacher to waive their administrative rights. In this way, the learners themselves become administrators, responsible persons who can request more and provide more support as a collective than a single person ever could. Furthermore, the teachers save themselves from the unnecessary burden of tedious maintenance work, which arises from the fact that they have more rights and consequently more duties. Besides such exclusive rights, any passwords and similar access restrictions should also be removed as far as possible. What happens in the classroom can safely be made publicly available. Furthermore, the simpler the access to the system, the greater the acceptance by learners. The corresponding files should be easily locatable, with a single click if possible (e.g., via a TinyURL).[3] In this context, the impression should not be given that the system is universal and final. The average half-life of hardware and software applications fell below the duration of long-term and short-term secondary school long ago. Thus, a flexible change of platform may be imposed for media education, but also for practical reasons. Finally, the flexibility of teaching is further optimized when all participants have access to (mobile) computers with a (wireless) Internet connection at all times. The ever-increasing availability of the latest generation of Netbooks suggests that they should be declared obligatory for secondary school in the same way as the calculator.

THE INTERNAL PROJECTS

In principle, internal wiki projects can be clearly distinguished from external wiki projects. In general, internal projects are publicly accessible via the URL, but are primarily implemented for internal use in the context of the curriculum. In contrast, external projects take the form of mature products, which are aimed at the general public and all German-speaking Internet users, for example, in the form of a Wikipedia article.

The Working Texts

First of all, the following should be noted. There is rarely a text written in German classes which would not benefit from being published in a wiki. Paradoxically, this is initially true for ephemeral homework texts. While all learners have to complete the respective assignments on their personal, centrally linked page before a certain deadline, the tiresome issue of checking homework almost resolves itself. In this respect, the automatic wiki notification systems[4] provide valuable services. However, the benefits for teachers reach further: On the basis of the existing work, they can specifically prepare the following lessons, instead of being at the mercy of the emerging results on the deadline day. Thus, they can prepare a selection of relevant text excerpts in advance almost without any effort, or demonstrate the aspects of a school project which have clearly caused problems, as required. The personal homework wiki also brings benefits for the learners: the knowledge that the teacher will be automatically informed about the completion of the work assignments releases them from any speculation that it will not be noticed if they do not complete the assignments. Furthermore, it is exciting and motivating to be able to browse the work of classmates and to know that this is also possible in the opposite direction. With regard to the publication, the learners are also encouraged to make the ostensibly private texts less informal: in the knowledge that the text will be publicly accessible, it happens, more or less of their own accord, that they express themselves more carefully, they make fewer mistakes, and they get to the heart of their project.

Continuous writing skills training is virtually automated with the homework wiki. Finally, it is clear that the digital collection of all work assignments can be more flexibly managed and more easily processed, for example, for examinations, than a hodgepodge of notes.

It is just a small step from here to a digital work journal, a medium that comprehensively illustrates the individual thought processes of the learners in lessons. In addition to homework, lesson notes, and work assignments, questions and reflections as well as considerations independent from the daily routine could be integrated. The concept of dialogical learning,[5] the continuous didactic written dialogue between teacher and learners, can be put into practice with a digital journal in wiki form just as easily as with a booklet written by hand. The benefit of the consistent digitalization of the journal is that the teacher is no longer the only other party whom the learners can address: due to the complete transparency of all content, they can all become dialogue partners for each other, whereby they comment on, supplement, acknowledge, or assess each other's work journals. It is clear that the otherwise exponentially growing effort required from the teacher for commentary and assessment can be minimized to an acceptable level by this process. Furthermore, such a digital work journal can be a meaningful basis for performance assessment with the correspondingly communicated assessment criteria.

Finally, the same benefits are also available if other long-term written assignments are moved to digital environments. In particular, reading journals or writing workshops can be advantageously operated in the form of a wiki. There will immediately be more transparency, more publicity, and more didactic scope.

The iBoard

The blackboard has always been central to teaching. The traditional green-board and the modern whiteboard have received competition in recent years from their electronic counterpart, which has removed them from more and more classrooms. If this article proposes the *digital blackboard* as a radical new interpretation of the blackboard, then it is not to replace the other forms, but rather to expand the methodological range by one medium that offers three remarkable benefits. Thus, unlike conventional boards, the digital blackboard is not bound to a certain classroom, but rather it can project at any given location and it can be modified at will. Furthermore, the digital board can be "cleaned" at the push of a button at any time, and the old board images are automatically stored. And finally, the handling has been dynamized: instead of the teacher or a single person from the class, the entire group can write on the board, both simultaneously and in real time.

As significant as this innovation sounds, its implementation is just as simple. In this respect, nothing is more necessary[6] than a URL and a digital document, such as a Google Doc,[7] that allows collaborative writing. In this way, the teacher can set up a forum for everyone involved without prior knowledge; a digital plenum, which can combine the individual considerations of all class members in no time, rather than a few individual opinions. This digital blackboard has proved particularly valuable when as many ideas, questions, opinions, or proposals for solutions as possible need to be gathered from all participants within a very short period of time. However, it also provides excellent services with regard to longer work processes, as demonstrated in the following model sequence:

1. The learners receive or submit an—advantageously collaborative—assignment (e.g., examine a different guiding principle of the text, use a different method of interpretation).
2. They prepare this assignment in their digital work journal.
3. They acknowledge, discuss, and modify their individual proposals for solution in writing in groups.
4. They copy their results to the digital blackboard. The teacher advantageously prepares a table with the necessary number of cells for this purpose. Thus, they can ensure a clear arrangement and avoid losing cursors or views of the user interface.
5. The class acknowledges, discusses, and modifies the results as required in plenary, moderated by the respective groups.
6. If relevant, the teacher or respective groups may move the agreed results to a separate document that will be centrally linked and possibly write-protected. The collection of such documents can serve as the basis for examination or examination preparation.

In this way, the work processes of all participants are stored in layers like a palimpsest and thus they form the ever-growing knowledge store of the entire group. An ostensibly blank sheet remains on the surface, ready for new challenges.

The Texts

In both theory and practice, the secondary school teaching of writing has, as indicated above, established the belief that process-oriented work on one's own texts is crucial for the sustainable development of writing skills. Wikis are an ideal medium for the documentation and organization of this longer-term writing process from the initial idea through mutual feedback to the final version. With their synthesis of flexibility and stability, they provide the optimal basis for the learners to work on a simultaneously stable and flexible product for longer periods. In this respect, they collect all individual working phases and thus they document the origin of the text, whereby they date, meaningfully title, and organize the different versions of text and commentaries in descending chronological order. In this way, the editorial wiki can serve as a basis for the assessment of the work process by the teacher. This can be divided into the following broad stages:

1. The learners receive a challenging writing task that spurs them on to perfection (e.g., science fiction short story based around an ancient heroic figure; essay about the future of the secondary school).
2. They develop initial ideas for their text in the form of clusters and mind-maps. They can realize these on paper, locally on their PC[8] or online and interactively in cooperation with other learners.[9] Both of the last-mentioned possibilities have the advantage that they are easier to integrate in the editorial wiki as image files. Furthermore, the creative chaos of the intuitive-spontaneous cluster can be transferred to the clear arrangement of an ordered mind-map almost without any effort, then in the fixed form of a writing plan. Text ideas can be developed in this media continuum without self-censorship and form an increasingly stable construction in flowing transitions.
3. The learners develop a raw text, the first draft, in their personal editorial wiki from the (visualized) writing plan or independently. The primitive user interface of the wiki is particularly suitable for this raw version, as it has no distractive potential other than a few formatting options.[10] Synonym suggestions are notably absent, so too are suggestions for spelling and grammar, not to mention the mass of layout decisions which deflect from the primary task of text production. This artificial limitation also involves the fact that there is only a short period of time available for the first draft (e.g., 30 or 60 minutes). In

this way, a raw text is created in a form of écriture *automatique*, which is already viable and clearly has the essential characteristics of the end product, such as elements that require revision.

4. The learners group together in tandems and annotate on each other's raw versions. In this respect, a wide variety of feedback settings are conceivable. In this initial feedback phase, it is crucial that the commentary is limited to specific but central aspects, it is constructive and motivating, and it is in written form.[11]

5. The class can analyze the feedback texts on the digital blackboard in plenary and collectively reduce the number of guiding principles. If the teacher moves these guiding principles to a separate document and places so-called anchors, the learners can subsequently link to their feedback with the corresponding anchor points and thus make their opinion even more transparent.

6. Based on the written feedback from fellow students and the guiding concepts developed in plenary, the learners revise their own raw versions. In this respect, it makes no difference whether they do this directly in the editorial wiki or initially in a conventional or unconventional[12] word-processing program, from which they export the text into the wiki at the end.

7. Steps 5 and 6 can be repeated as required. With regard to larger text assignments, the cooperation between two partners can be institutionalized as so-called tandem writing. These partners agree on workloads, feedback cycles, and further guidelines for feedback.[13]

8. Of course, the teacher can also give his or her constructive feedback in an advanced stage of the text.[14]

9. The end result is published in perfect formatting in the editorial Wiki.

10. With regard to the assessment of the end results, the teacher can also involve the learners (the same class or, better still, another class) in the context of an anonymous online survey.[15]

THE EXTERNAL PROJECTS

The fruits of this lengthy editorial ripening process deserve to be showcased and presented for the consumption of a wider public. This can take the form of simple websites which are linked to each other and which adapt to the published content in terms of design.[16] In order to ensure the continuity of the work process, it may well make sense to ultimately publish the products developed in editorial wikis in the wiki format. Both practical and aesthetically pleasing designs are also possible with a wiki, which the learners are familiar with from the outset from their daily use of the medium. Two such wiki showcases will now be introduced in model cases.

The Digital Museum

In the context of a multidisciplinary, cross-lingual, and inter-school project, a small digital museum was created in 2004 by three classes from the Neuen Kantonsschule Aarau with the Aargauischen Kunsthaus and a French class from the Alten Kantonsschule Aarau. Eighty-three young people each presented their personal favorite piece on one page in the form of a subjective text in German and French. Each page is supplemented by a photograph, which shows the writer in front of their painting. The learners developed their text in a multistage revision and feedback process, as outlined above, and after several visits to the Aargauischen Kunsthaus. The work was completed by the small website www.wortbild.ch.vu on the one hand, and a public vernissage of the website on the other hand, in which the learners presented their pieces to the numerous audience members in attendance—individually at first, then in a simultaneous cacophony of more than eighty voices. In this respect, the simplicity of the implementation and the integrative nature of the project, which combined the aesthetic, media, and linguistic elements as if by itself, is more remarkable than the aesthetic quality of the resulting texts or photographs.

The Lyric Lexicon

Wikis, with their intuitive automatic linking mechanism, are particularly well suited for the development of small special lexicons. Thus, a lyric lexicon was created at the Neuen Kantonsschule Aarau between 2006 and 2008, which is still accessible in a beta version at www.erlesen.ch.vu. In this respect, the learners were given the task of selecting any poem printed in one of the widely read anthologies, and presenting it by observing a certain structure.

The learners had to use a digital template, which defined certain key parameters in info boxes. This was automatically linked to the main document, so as to create a lexicon, a continually expanding list of poems, which can be sorted by author, poem title, length, theme, and so on with just one mouse-click. In the end, the project was so successful that it was taken over by the hep publishing house in Bern in 2009 and it has been operated under the URL www.lyrikonline.ch ever since.

The Wikipedia Articles

Thus, wiki sets a precedent, and this applies all the more to the most prominent wiki by far: the encyclopedia Wikipedia. In the meantime, not one school day passes without the average Swiss secondary school student clicking on at least one page for school purposes. Instead of criticizing this consumerist use of allegedly dubious scientific sources and suppressing the use of Wikipedia in classes, perhaps the teachers would be better advised to take the bull by the horns and to combat the inadequacies of Wikipedia from the other side:

through active cooperation on the encyclopedia. In any case, it is hard to see why the knowledge accumulated in secondary school classes is always filed away. Why not professionally prepare the intellectual capital and simultaneously reinvest it in a collective educational establishment, from which all German-speaking users could profit?

In this respect, the fact that there is already a Wikipedia page concerning a particular area or a literary work should have little effect on the collective drive for research. Thus, it is possible to supplement existing articles by certain dimensions, to correct incorrect or half-correct statements and to provide the statements with illustrative supporting documents. For example, the existing articles concerning Daniel Kehlmann's novel *Ruhm*[17] and Plenzdorf's *Neuen Leiden des jungen W.* were considerably enhanced by the learners in collaboration, whereby they systematically supplemented the aspects of significance and made editorial revisions. Of course, it is more rewarding to completely redesign articles, as in the case of the contribution to Tucholsky's *Rheinsberg* [18] In principle, all subjects in secondary school German classes can be processed in Wikipedia articles. The core discipline of the subject, the analysis of different literary works, proved to be particularly suitable, above all, naturally, when the works are relatively new or rather unknown. With regard to work on the encyclopedia in German classes, the following points should be observed:

1. First, the teacher must familiarize themselves with their requirements. Only people with experience in the editing of articles can give a qualified introduction to a class. The latter is an important basic requirement for positive cooperation and collaboration. Learners can learn a lot through self-study or *learning by doing,* but not everything. In any case, the guiding and organizing hand of the teacher or another coordinating authority is necessary. Furthermore, it can make sense to start a mentor program[19] with the class in advance, as has been the case since 2007.

2. Once all learners are familiar with the conditions of use of the encyclopedia and committed to its fundamental values, someone opens a Wikipedia account on behalf of the class with a meaningful user name, which will encompass the subsequent contributions.[20]

3. As regards the contents of the work, it is initially a question of taking note of the current state of research in respect of scientific conventionalism. This includes, for instance, checking whether there is a Wikipedia entry and, if so, its current status. Based on this appraisal, the research work tasks can be determined and allocated. In this respect, a collaborative approach is recommended; for instance, a modified puzzle technique has proved successful, whereby the different members are assigned the same task and work on the task individually, before exchanging information with the other group members and summarizing their results in a collective short text. In principle, it is possible

for a class to carry out research work, which exceeds the capacity of individual Wikipedia experts, in this manner within a short period of time.

4. The results of both the subgroup and the entire class can initially be established in an internal wiki or on the digital blackboard. In doing so, it is possible to view, annotate, and, if necessary, revise the results of partner groups at different times.

5. Once the articles are more or less finalized, the learners should incorporate them in a separate test document in their own user accounts. In principle, any number of these subpages can be created[21] and then deleted after use. If it is an existing article that is being extended or changed, a working copy, identified as such, should be made in advance[22] using the corresponding template.[23] This transfer has the advantage that the final text does not then need to be painstakingly "translated" into Wikipedia syntax by one person, usually the teacher. Instead, the learners are required to solve all simple programming problems themselves.

6. Once the text has been viewed by the groups and finally by the teacher, and it has been approved by the collective, it can be copied to the official Wikipedia. In this respect, it is recommended that the teacher or someone from the class make a small contribution to the discussion page to briefly comment on the entry or the amendments.

The Wikipedia collaboration with secondary school classes is as simple as it is advantageous. First, the learners find out firsthand about the reliability of Wikipedia, and thus they learn to better assess the relevance of individual articles. In practical terms, they become familiar with the individual mechanisms which are normal for the creation of a Wikipedia article, and they must learn to assert themselves in the hustle and bustle, which is often fraught with difficulties. Furthermore, the work on Wikipedia articles is optimal propaedeutic practice for university research, in particular for academic written discourse. The numerous contributions to the encyclopedia do not meet scientific requirements, but the publication standards are stringent enough for secondary school. In particular, the prescribed objectivity of the presentation, the detailed formal instructions, and the requirement to verify all statements by making appropriate references to the (secondary) literature present an ideal challenge for future academics. Furthermore, it is clear that the prospect of making one's little contributions to the global encyclopedia inspires the learners. And finally, the finished Wikipedia article can provide a framework for exam preparation. Thus, a process that is common practice at secondary school is legitimized. A student who became aware of this phenomenon mischievously said: "Now we can do it officially!"

NOTES

1. Wiki or wikiwiki in Hawaiian essentially means "fast" or "quickly."
2. See, for example, Kruse, Berger and Ulmi (2006); Fix (2008).
3. With the service of www.tinyurl.com, a mini-version can be created from a URL of any size in no time. The URL can be designed for free with the forwarding service of www.nic.ch.vu with just a bit more effort.
4. For example, the Wikipedia watch list or the TWiki Web Changes Notification Service.
5. See Ruf and Gallin (2005).
6. Of course, a projector and a sufficient number of computers are also required.
7. Furthermore, the successor products of the EtherPad software acquired by Google are suitable, for example, PiratePad (http://piratepad.net) or PrimaryPad (http://primarypad.com).
8. For example, with the software FreeMind; see http://freemind.sourceforge.net/wiki/index.php/Main_Page.
9. For example, with the browser application Mind24; see http://mind42.com.
10. However, the learners must be encouraged to regularly save their files, as wikis do not normally have an automatic save function in contrast to Google Docs.
11. As is generally known, vocal negative global criticism ("I don't understand this," "I don't like such texts") has a devastating effect on the motivation to write. See Kruse (2007), pp. 251ff.; and Wolfsberger (2009), pp. 208–9.
12. Apple's minimalist text editor iA Writer (see www.iawriter.com) or the freeware WriteMonkey (http://writemonkey.com) offer a puristic writing medium without any frills.
13. More information on tandem writing can be found in Knaus (2009), p. 22.
14. This assistance is provided in the context of the scaffolding concept; thus the teacher accompanies and safeguards the independent development work of the learners with a "scaffold" as required. The assessment of the assistance or its classification in the context of process assessment is measured in terms of the quality of the source text: the higher the quality of the annotated text, the more differentiated the corresponding feedback.
15. For example. the surveys of Google Docs (www.docs.google.com). All learners award 0 to 5 points for each text based on the initially defined criteria, so that there is an overall assessment in the form of a grade for all workers in the end. The teacher may include this in part or in full in their own assessment as required.
16. In the meantime, a countless number of free providers have established themselves on the market, which also allow laymen to design appealing layouts without disturbing advertisements, e.g., Google Sites (www.sites.google.com) or Jimdo (www.de.jimdo.com).
17. http://de.wikipedia.org/wiki/Ruhm_%28Roman%29; Wikipedia: http://de.wikipedia.org/wiki/Benutzer_Diskussion:Infcom09/Baustelle.

18. Wikipedia: http://de.wikipedia.org/wiki/Rheinsberg:_Ein_Bilderbuch_f%C3 %BCr_Verliebte.

19. Wikipedia: http://de.wikipedia.org/wiki/Wikipedia:Mentorenprogramm/R%C3 %BCckblick.

20. In this respect, keen class members remain free to create individual accounts. It is much clearer for the administrators of Wikipedia if they have to deal with one single contact partner, rather than twenty.

21. Per sample: Wikipedia: http://de.wikipedia.org/wiki/Benutzer:XYZ/ Artikelname.

22. Wikipedia: http://de.wikipedia.org/wiki/Wikipedia:Urheberrechte_beachten #Artikel_verschie-ben.2C_Artikel_zusammenf.C3.BChren.2C_Artikel_aufteilen .2C_Arbeitskopien.

23. http://de.wikipedia.org/wiki/Vorlage:Tempor%C3 %A4rkopie. Note: "This text is a temporary working copy of the article . . . "

REFERENCES

Fix, M. "Texte schreiben." 2008. In *Schreibprozesse im Deutschunterricht*. 2nd edition. Paderborn: Schöningh.

Knaus, B. 2009. *Einfach schreiben: Deutsch am Gymnasium 2*. Rothenburg: Fuchs.

Kruse, O. 2007. *Keine Angst vor dem leeren Blatt: Ohne Schreibblockaden durchs Studium*. Campus: Frankfurt.

Kruse, O., K. Berger, and M. Ulmi, eds. 2006. *Prozessorientierte Schreibdidaktik: Schreibtraining für Schule, Studium und Beruf*. Bern: Haupt.

Ruf, U., and P. Gallin. 2005. *Dialogisches Lernen in Sprache und Mathematik*. Seelze-Velber: Kallmeyer.

Wolfsberger, J. 2009. *Frei geschrieben: Mut, Freiheit & Strategie für wissenschaftliche Abschlussarbeiten*. 2nd edition. Vienna: UTB/Böhlau.

NIKLAUS SCHATZMANN

12
Using Wikis for School Management

THE INTRODUCTION OF INNOVATIONS IS USUALLY TRIGGERED by existing deficiencies on one hand, and the availability of a new solution that can correct such deficiencies and offer new possibilities on the other hand. The difficulty lies in striking the right balance. Technical and administrative expenses, as well as the ever-present diverse emotional resistance to such changes have to be considered. After taking all factors into account, a mixed form between the old and new can create a radical departure from the status quo. The introduction of a wiki in our secondary school as a platform for management of the school's primary information, with an audience of parents and outside community members, took place under such circumstances. As with all technical innovations, the question of training the target user groups arose. Many years after its initial establishment, our wiki remains a functional and well-used platform today for management of school information.

THE STARTING POINT

In early 2003, our secondary school launched its first professional website (previously there had been a website created by the students, but it was seldom updated and not very informative). At that time, not all the secondary schools in our canton had a website. It was astonishing to see how quickly our school pushed the limits and began an expansion of website services in this direction. Our major problems owed primarily to the sluggishness of the system on two levels:

1. The school made a conscious decision to not let the website be created by a few "computer geeks" at school, but opted for this to be handled by a professional website company which was tasked with providing a compelling design and ensuring the operation remained trouble-free. Since programming of a website back then was time-consuming, the company was also responsible for the ongoing updates of the website. The school administration, which wanted to use the website as a "business card" and a quick way of offering information, soon found the update procedure too cumbersome and slow. The colorful elements of school life (such as photos and descriptions of school events) also involved huge programming efforts and corresponding costs.

2. With the introduction of e-mail addresses to all members of the school (teachers, staff, and students) in 2004, the use of ICT, especially digital communication, increased abruptly. Deficiencies became more apparent in the area of ICT literacy, which required the provision of ICT skills to students in the form of modularized units in various school subjects.[1]

In addition to these technical-pedagogical shortcomings, issues of data protection also become the focus of our considerations: to what extent could a person put the pictures of school members onto the Internet without obtaining permission? On the other hand, how could we satisfy the need, especially among young people, for such pictures of class and school events?

FIRST WIKI EXPERIENCES: PURE EUPHORIA

Back then, wiki was an interesting, albeit largely unknown platform at the school. In our case, it was the know-how and the enthusiasm of one individual that largely shaped our wiki usage from the beginning until today. A history teacher who had worked with wiki on his own for some time approached the school board with an offer to build a wiki platform for the school and to take care of it. In 2005 the experimental platform was launched.

These first experiences can only be described as, in a way, euphoric. The author of this overview, at that time a secondary school history teacher, was also responsible for the public relations of the school. For the first time, it was possible to publish simple information for the whole school and individual classes, and above all, to customize, correct, and provide supplements quickly. In turn, the students were given the opportunity to present themselves on class web pages and connect to one another. To us at that time, it seemed impressive, especially given the completely new options for learners to establish real cooperation on the wiki among themselves and with teachers. Engagement and greater interaction among the school/home community in this online context was supported and it was exciting to witness this unfolding.

In this context, an important question for the further development of our wiki arose: how should we assign authorial rights? We decided for the principle of the greatest possible freedom. With very few exceptions, all members of the school are allowed to edit all pages. These pages are hidden from search engines, but otherwise they are freely accessible. The risk of unwanted manipulations of wiki pages (i.e., student jokes) was offset by the educational value and the promotion of rational and responsible use of the Internet.

After seven years of operating the platform, we can say with relief that favoring freedom has proven useful. The changing history of our wiki is monitored by our wiki moderator with a close eye, but there is not enough time for a complete review of all abnormalities. Nevertheless, problems have only occurred very occasionally and generally appeared at the beginning of the implementation in the form of deliberate changes to sections that were then disagreed upon. These were all quite harmless and could be remedied after private conversations. Social controls evidently play a very important role and can prevent mischief from individual students. Our wiki remained largely unaffected by problems such as cyberbullying and inappropriate self-presentations. The reasons were certainly diverse, and self-responsibility and awareness-raising events with our first classes appear to have played their part. Also, it may be that students with problematic Internet behavior tend to avoid such platforms, instead opting for greater anonymity.

PROBLEMS OF DEFINITION

In the meantime, our consistently positive experience with the wiki resulted in the consideration that perhaps the official website of our school should be given up in favor of a wiki.

The favoring of this consideration showed that there were problems of definition between the two platforms in everyday use. Specifically, a user was no longer sure about which information could be found on the school website or on the wiki site. Above all, not only the school board, but many commissions and working groups (i.e., normal teachers) also preferred (and still prefer) to use the wiki as an easier way to provide information, bypassing the webmaster in the process. This behavior can be related mainly to the cuts to expenses in schools, so that a large part of school events organization is delegated to the teachers, and some even to the students. A specific example would be our annual sports day, where over ten student leaders, under the direction of two physical education teachers, are responsible for the organization of their respective fields. With the use of a wiki, it is possible for those responsible to compile and publish important basic information (maps, schedules, group organizations, etc.) as well as specific information for different events (materials required, group meetings, fixtures, etc.). Here, the wiki has effectively replaced and supplemented the school notice board in an efficient and timely manner, allowing for easy updating and also access from the parents.

On the other hand, with the transition to an expanded wiki operation, the advantages of a purely internal wiki have to be clarified. Currently, relatively strict rules are applied in relation to data protection, and therefore the student photos are made deliberately small, published in poor resolution and low numbers. This is not compatible with the needs of our students, especially those in the lower forms who like to take pictures on school trips and excursions, and sit together later to comment on them. Also, the information provided by the teachers in the subject pages could easily be accessed by the whole world, which might result in problems with the working material such as copyright issues.

As a result, along with the decision to definitely establish the school wiki, a web concept and documented policy plan for the school web presence, maintaining both platforms, was developed in 2006. The web concept has proven successful and is largely unchanged in its function. The concept basically adheres the two web presences (the school website and wiki platform). However, a redesign of the home page was also initiated, in order to ensure a clear division of responsibilities between the two sites and a straightforward operability of the school website. New technologies were also used, which allowed for updating of the website through an internal webmaster. This is an important element of the wiki philosophy that has contributed to the school website.

The web concept developed in the secondary school will be presented briefly below.

THE SIMPLE WEB CONCEPT PLAN FOR THE SECONDARY SCHOOL

- The school uses the Internet to communicate internally and externally. In order to cover various needs as much as possible, two main sites with a total of five sub-areas are maintained.
- Each area has its own specific target group and content. Overlapping is avoided whenever possible.

- Pages and sections of all internal sub-areas can be connected to one another through the use of links, forming a suitable network for future-oriented knowledge management (see figure 12.1).

A) www..ch	
• is the official website of the school with a uniform layout and strictly hierarchical navigation • deliberately avoids having too many pictures • is maintained by the Information Officer of the school, and supported by an external company	
A1) www..ch (external)	**A2)** www..ch (internal)
The official "showcase" of the school; contains content for the public at large • also serves as an advertising medium for our school • contains official information written by the education department and the school management/administration	Provides information for all members of the school (password protected with different access rights) • contains official content with a certain degree of confidentiality (class lists, addresses, internal documents) • Provides access to e-mail and weekly schedules for all members of the school

B) Website		
• A somewhat freer communication platform of the school. • Can be edited by all registered users of the school, and therefore functions only when respect and a sense of responsibility are generally observed and promoted. • Is promoted as a platform for the exchange of information and views, with the accompanying measures applied: Training of all users in the context of ICT literacy, teacher training, mutual support during use, Wiki support hours, feedback between users, written commitment of all students for responsible use, control of webpages by the teachers, control of ICT core teams, punishment for improper use. • Can be theoretically seen by any Internet user, but is not found by Internet search engines. • Is maintained by external Wiki specialists in cooperation with the personnel responsible for the Wiki in school.		
B1) Pages of the student body	**B2)** Pages of classes/ students	**B3)** Pages of the departments/teachers
• Contains content that concerns more than one class or more than one department but are not official information of the school management or administration	• Are the main communication platform for students in the same class • Are also "showcases" of individual classes for all members of the school	• Are platforms for communication within the same department • Contain information concerning the subjects for all students

FIGURE 12.1

Characterization of the websites and their functions.

SCHOOL WIKI 2005 TO 2011: CONCLUSION AND OUTLOOK

After six years of operations, the school wiki had 11,939 pages in July 2011. This number says quite a bit about the success of the platform.

Quite significantly, the teachers should be credited for making themselves familiar with the new working tool without reservations and integrating it into the classroom. Without the support of the teachers, the wiki would not be able to achieve its current success. By looking at the web log, it is evident that it is mainly the teachers who maintain the exchanges.

The wiki has lost much of its importance as class communication pages. In the early days of our wiki, these pages were the medium for informal exchanges between the students. Blog features were extensively used, especially in the lower forms. This use has since then declined. It is obvious that a large part of these exchanges have shifted to forums such as Facebook or Twitter, which were not available or accessible back then. In light of these new online services, which are more modern in many aspects, the usage of our internal pages is still surprisingly high. Whether this is owing to a conscious rejection of other forums due to the wiki's anonymity and complex privacy settings remains undetermined based on the current user behavior.

Furthermore, the wiki has an extremely high and ever-increasing importance for the teachers. They continue to make their teaching material available as "archives" for the classes and also as "self-learning" in the download area for lesson units.

The wiki also offers the simplest technical solution for several people to interact. Information can be provided by the teachers or commissions and supplemented by others (such as a registration list for internal school events), and different people can provide various information for events (such as project weeks with different students in charge).

Finally, the wiki is also considered as the semiofficial photo database. It has the advantage that different users can share their own photos by uploading them to a shared page without having to register at external services.

How will our wiki evolve over the next few years? From today's perspective, there is still no alternative with a similarly efficient cost-benefit ratio. Certainly there are many individual applications today that offer more comfortable services and functions that a classical wiki lacks, such as tools for the automatic control of learning objectives. Our wiki is also lagging far behind more modern cloud services. At the time of writing this chapter, it is still necessary to upload each picture individually and reduce its size if necessary, in contrast to other online services that enable automated uploading of image galleries with just one click.

In short, there are no services that can cover the various usages of wiki in such a compact and consistent way. No platforms can claim such a high degree of commitment, reliability, and trustworthiness as the wiki, no matter how sophisticated their tools may be. Thanks to its openness, the wiki can be customized entirely to meet our needs.

With this in mind, it must be noted that the digital world has indeed progressed a lot since the initial implementation we report in this overview, but there is still no alternative solution that replaces the wiki for the purposes described. Based on our positive experiences, it would take a lot of convincing for us to give up our wiki and all of the constructive and creative uses it has realized for our school.

NOTE

1. For our work with ICT literacies, the school won an award in the WBZ-Competition "Informatik als Instrument in den einzelnen Fachunterricht integriert" in 2008.

BEAT DÖBELI HONEGGER
AND MICHELE NOTARI

13

How to Find the Best Wiki for Varying Purposes

IF YOU WANT TO WORK WITH A WIKI IN THE CLASSROOM, YOU will be spoiled for choice. It is just not possible to count the number of options now available. Is it worth the effort of setting up your own wiki server, or is it better to license one or even employ one for free? Perhaps it makes more sense to use the wiki provided by the learning management system (LMS) implemented already in your school. This chapter offers some up-to-date decision-making help for selecting your own wiki platform for a classroom project.

SPOILED FOR CHOICE

In the case of classic text processing, the decision to use a specific tool can be made relatively quickly. The number of common products that can be installed on your computer is limited, and the number of text processors available online can be counted on one hand only. However, the choice is more difficult to make when it comes to wikis. There are many more concrete products available, and unlike word processors, there isn't a common data format for these products, so it takes significant effort to transfer the content from one wiki to another. The choice of a wiki should therefore be carefully considered. When being used for classroom projects, the following questions are particularly relevant:

- What goals will be achieved with the use of the wiki?
- Which functionalities must the future wiki feature?
- Who should be able to edit the wiki, and who should be allowed to view it?
- What language and media skills do the learners possess?

CLASSIC WIKI OR WIKI-LIKE?

In recent years, various systems have been developed that exhibit certain characteristics of wikis, while others do not show such similarities at all. Depending on the objectives of the planned use in teaching, it might not make sense to use a classic wiki anymore, and wiki-like tools may be more suitable. These tools can cover the needed functionalities better and are easier to use, since the unnecessary functions are not included.

Currently, wiki-like systems that do not offer hypertext links between different documents, but allow multiple users to work on the same document simultaneously, are particularly widespread. The first such web-based system was launched under the name of EtherPad in 2008. This software was acquired by Google in 2009 and integrated into the functionality of the online word processor Google Docs. Due to protests from the Internet community, the original EtherPad server on Google was shut down and the former version of the software was published under an open source license, which made available a variety of EtherPad servers today, and allows other online word processors to edit the same document simultaneously. The systems can be roughly divided into the following two types:

1. Plain text editors allow only the editing of text and feature minimum formatting possibilities. The inclusion of pictures and graphics is not possible, and the system's focus is on the content and structure, not the layout.
2. Developed word processors cover a large part of the daily required word-processing functions and allow the inclusion of pictures and graphics. With greater layout options and functions such as footnotes and tables of contents, these developed word processors have the potential to replace the ones installed on the computer.

Plain text editors appear to be more suitable when a raw text is to be rapidly created together by a group, or a list (of questions, books, links, etc.) is to be made, or a brainstorming session is to be conducted. In the simplest case, the URL can be published on the classroom board, by e-mail or in the form of a 2D-bar code on the projector, and everyone involved can work on one or more documents individually or in groups.

The possibility for simultaneous editing is certainly the biggest advantage over traditional wikis, which do not offer this feature. In addition, as the students are already familiar with known text processors, the time required to learn the functions of the tool will decrease, while the link functions of classical wikis have to be first comprehended by most of the students before use.

"... IS A WIKI" OR "... HAS A WIKI"?

The consideration of whether a classic wiki shall be used in a learning scenario brings up the question of whether the corresponding functions are already available in the school. Many learning management systems offer Wikis as part of their tool palette. It is therefore natural to use the wiki already available in the implemented LMS, instead of evaluating and configuring a separate tool. The advantages are obvious: the learners are already involved in the existing system and are familiar with it.

There are several reasons why "... has a Wiki" is not the same as "... is a Wiki":

Lack of accessibility to outsiders: the wikis in an LMS are usually not accessible to outsiders. Therefore, they are not designed for teaching scenarios in which the work should be made accessible to a broader audience, and they do not even allow participation from others. An attempted collaboration of two classes from different schools has already resulted in tedious administrative work.

Reduced functionality and ease of use: the Wiki engines are often not integrated into an LMS, but the LMS developers will program a separate wiki (for example, Educanet2). The functionality and ease of use of an integrated wiki is usually worse when compared to a stand-alone wiki.

Controlled LMS structures contradict the lack of structure of the wikis: wikis and learning management systems represent opposing concepts. There is usually a clear distinction between teachers and students in an LMS, where all rights are laid out in detail and there is a special tool available for every possible application. A wiki, however, adheres to its original philosophy of being unregulated and unstructured. It is questionable whether the basic ideas of a wiki can develop fully in a structured LMS.

WHICH WIKI SHOULD BE CHOSEN?

If the decision is made to select a classic stand-alone wiki, then the question of a suitable wiki engine should next be considered. In early 2013, over a hundred different Wiki engines were listed on the comparison platform www.wikimatrix.org. The selections range from minimalistic versions that make do with a single file, to huge systems that are suitable for large, global organizations. There exist wiki engines for all kinds of operating systems, in all possible programming languages. In particular, if a longer or more intensive use of the wiki is scheduled, the choice should be considered carefully, because data transfer between different wiki engines is rarely possible and users will be reluctant to learn a new user interface and wiki syntax. Before introducing three well-established wiki engines that can be used for bigger and lengthier wiki projects, here are some criteria for selecting a suitable wiki engine for teaching and learning purposes:

Usability according to the level. Depending on the school level and the media skills of the users, there will be different demands on the usability of the wiki engine. Most wiki engines feature a WYSIWYG editor that enables users to edit pages without using any codes.

Interface language. Not all wiki engines can provide a user interface in German. Depending on the language skills of the learners, this can pose an obstacle to usage.

Multimedia integration. Based on the intended use, the integration of multimedia content is an important functionality of the wiki. It is important to pay attention to how easy the integration is, and whether the multimedia files are held on the wiki server or on other servers (YouTube, Flickr etc.).

Extendibility through plug-ins. Some Wiki engines can be extended by installing plug-ins. As a result, the lack of structure in wikis can be supplemented by specific structures (calendars, spreadsheets, whiteboards, etc.). If a wiki server is to be used longer and for a variety of projects, such extendibility may be desired or even become necessary.

Availability on the desired server. Finally, it must be ensured that the selected wiki engine can also be installed on the planned, or already available, server.

Connects to the existing user management. If a wiki is to be operated for a long period with protected access, the availability of accessing existing data for the teachers and students will be desired (so-called single sign-ons). For this, the wiki engine must offer assistance.

Four comprehensive wiki engines are currently (in 2015) available for bigger and lengthier wiki projects:

- **MediaWiki** (www.mediawiki.org) is a free, PHP-based wiki engine which is used on Wikipedia and was developed specifically for the needs of Wikipedia. This is both an advantage and a disadvantage. Due to Wikipedia's popularity and its widespread applications, the user interface is well known to many users. This can increase the level of acceptance and reduce training time. However, MediaWiki is primarily geared to the needs of a large, multilingual lexicon, which does not necessarily coincide with the needs of a learning environment. Also, the current MediaWiki (in 2015) still does not feature a graphic editor.

- **DokuWiki** (www.dokuwiki.org) is a free PHP-based wiki engine which can be largely extended through plug-ins. Its strength lies particularly in the preparation of documentation and it is used by numerous school projects.

- **FosWiki** (www.foswiki.org) is a free Perl-based wiki engine which can be massively extended by plug-ins and is often used, especially in business and computer science-related environments. It is more complicated to operate than DokuWiki, but offers more options in its range of form-based processes and automations.

- **Wikispaces** (www.wikispaces.org) is not so extendable but offers a good ergonomy for learners and some adequate statists for the teacher.

SELF-HOSTING, RENTING, OR USING FREEWARE?

The question of choosing a suitable Wiki engine cannot be detached from the consideration of who is running the wiki, and of the computer where the wiki is to be run. In principle, there are three types of approaches: self-hosting, renting, or using free services on the Internet.

Self-Hosting Is Rarely Worth It

Self-hosting is usually not recommended for schools. A self-powered wiki server is worthwhile only if one wants to use the wiki over a longer term or on a larger scale. The teachers should focus on content and organizational issues and not have to deal with technical aspects of wiki use. One of the advantages of wikis is that they can usually be used without much technical know-how. However, for the teachers and students, this image is tarnished when wiki salespeople promote the latest technical advancements with shining eyes, but talk about update problems during the break. The self-hosting option is most highly recommended if specialized technicians can take over running the wiki.

Nonetheless, self-hosting is an interesting choice if the wiki can be run on a mobile computer. The teacher could then make his or her wiki available on his or her own notebook computer, connected to the local network, so that Internet access would not even be required. The wiki would then be available only during lessons, which is not a problem, or is even desired in certain scenarios. If the students have their own notebooks, netbooks, or tablets, small wiki engines could be implemented as a personal note-keeping system.

Wiki Renting

Generally, one would rather leave the technical operations to specialized companies that either have current wiki engines to offer, or have developed their own proprietary wiki engine. Data protection legislation and its conditions are to be considered when choosing a company in your own country or considering the best offers available in the world. Under certain circumstances, it is also possible for state agencies to take over wiki hosting and offer the service to respective educational institutions free of charge or at a cost price.

Free Wikis

Finally, there are a variety of free wiki offers on the Internet. What must be considered when choosing a wiki for rental applies to free wikis even more. Nobody guarantees that the wiki-hosting party will continue to exist in the future. The suitability of the offer also depends on the time horizon and the scope of the proposed use. If one needs the wiki only for a week, you would be more inclined to use freeware than somebody who is planning to invest a lot of time in a multiyear wiki project. Both rental and free wikis have a data export function, so that users can back up their data regularly, and the data will still be available even if the wiki host is suddenly gone.

Free wikis are often financed by advertisements, and some wikis offer the possibility of turning off the advertisements if the project is for educational purposes only. Today's web advertising is often context-sensitive. Thus, unsolicited advertisements might show up on a wiki with biology content. It is questionable whether content seamed with advertisements would be acceptable in a school context.

AND NOW?

We hope you will not be deterred by the diversity of wikis described in this chapter and will instead be motivated to start your own wiki project! Why not try using a free wiki first and get some experience? After that, you can decide whether wikis are part of your long-term work tools, and may choose to set up your own suitable wiki (or to let other professionals set it up for you).

More recent information on this book (especially short-lived references to questions posted here) can be found in the future, and not surprisingly, in a wiki at http://wikiway.ch.

Good luck!

Beat Döbeli Honegger and Michele Notari

About the Editors

MICHELE NOTARI is professor for educational technologies at the University of Teacher Education in Bern, Switzerland, and was an honorary assistant professor in the Faculty of Education, the University of Hong Kong. He has published articles in key journals in the area of technology-enhanced learning, along with a book and several book chapters related to collaborative learning using participative technologies. He is editor of a special edition of the *Journal of Educational Research and Evaluation* and is a board member of Wikisym (the international symposium on open collaboration), the international Conference on Mobile Learning, and the International Mobile Learning Festival. He holds a PhD in education, a master's degree in biology and computer sciences from the University of Berne, and a master's degree in educational technologies from the University of Geneva. His research focus is on using participative technologies for formative assessment and effective collaboration.

REBECCA REYNOLDS is an assistant professor of library and information science at the School of Communication and Information at Rutgers, the state university of New Jersey. Her research investigates middle- and high-school student inquiry, collaboration and creation during project-based learning with technology in schools, and the design of information systems to support successful learning outcomes. Her research is funded by an Institute for Museum and Library Services early career development grant. Her work has been published in many different conference proceedings and journals in the learning sciences and information sciences, and she has written a book coauthored with S. K. W. Chu and Michele Notari on inquiry-based learning. She holds a BA in sociology from Tufts University and an MA in media studies and Ph.D. in mass communication from Syracuse University, with postdoctoral work completed in information studies.

SAMUEL KAI WAH CHU is the head of division of information and technology studies and an associate professor at the Faculty of Education of the University of Hong Kong. He is also the deputy director (Centre for Information Technology in Education) in the Faculty of Education of that university. He has published over 170 articles and books, including key journals in the area of information and library science, information technology (IT) in education, school librarianship, academic librarianship, and knowledge management. He is also the author of a series of children's story books. Chu is the associate editor (Asia) for the *Online Information Review: The International Journal of Digital Information Research and Use.* He is also the Asia regional editor for the *Journal of Information & Knowledge Management.* Chu has obtained more than thirty research project grants with a total funding of more than one million dollars. His research interests cover the areas of twenty-first-century skills, social media in education, collaborative inquiry project-based learning, digital literacies, school and academic librarianship, game-based learning, and knowledge management and intellectual capital.

BEAT DÖBELI HONEGGER is professor at the Institute for Media and Schools at the Schwyz University of Teacher Education in Switzerland. He holds a PhD in computer science from the Swiss Federal Institute of Technology Zürich. His research interests cover all aspects of digital media in education: teaching and learning in the transition toward a digital society, strategic and operative information technology management in schools and universities, collaborative writing, digital textbooks, and the didactics of computer science.

Index